CIMA Exam Practice Kit

P3 — Performance Strategy

CIMA Exam Practice Kit

PUBLISHING

P3 – Performance Strategy

Teddy Foster

ELSEVIER

Amsterdam • Boston • Heidelberg • London • New York • Oxford
Paris • San Diego • San Francisco • Singapore • Sydney • Tokyo

CIMA Publishing
An imprint of Elsevier
Linacre House, Jordan Hill, Oxford OX2 8DP
30 Corporate Drive, Burlington, MA 01803

British Library Cataloguing in Publication Data
A catalogue record for this book is available from the British Library

Library of Congress Cataloging in Publication Data
A catalog record for this book is available from the Library of Congress

978-1-85617-738-2

For information on all CIMA publications
visit our website at www.elsevierdirect.com

Typeset by Macmillan Publishing Solutions
(www.macmillansolutions.com)

Printed and bound in Great Britain by CPI Antony Rowe, Chippenham, Wiltshire

10 11   11 10 9 8 7 6 5 4 3 2

Working together to grow
libraries in developing countries

www.elsevier.com | www.bookaid.org | www.sabre.org

ELSEVIER   BOOK AID
             International   Sabre Foundation

Contents

How To Use This Kit   vii
Syllabus Guidance, Learning Objectives and Verbs   ix
Learning Outcomes, Syllabus Content and Examination Format   xiii
Examination Techniques   xxv
Formulae   xxvii

Section 1: Theory Revision

1 **Introduction to Risk and Control**
   1.1 Introduction   3
   1.2 The emergence of risk, governance an control   5
   1.3 Corporate governance?   6
   1.4 Risk management   6
   1.5 Internal control?   7
   1.6 Audit?   7
   1.7 A model of governance, risk and control   7
   1.8 Fraud, information systems and financial risk   7

2 **Management Control Theory**   9
   Theory Highlights from CIMA Official Study System   11
   Theory Revision Questions   14
   Theory Revision Solutions   15

3 **Accounting Control and Behavioural Consequences**   21
   Theory Highlights from CIMA Official Study System   23
   Theory Revision Questions   25
   Theory Revision Solutions   27

4 **Corporate Governance and the Audit Committee**   33
   Theory Highlights from CIMA Official Study System   35
   Theory Revision Questions   37
   Theory Revision Solutions   38

5 **Risk and Risk Management**   43
   Theory Highlights from CIMA Official Study System   45
   Theory Revision Questions   48
   Theory Revision Solutions   50

6 Internal Control 61
Theory Highlights from CIMA Official Study System 63
Theory Revision Questions 65
Theory Revision Solutions 66

7 Internal Audit and the Auditing Process 71
Theory Highlights from CIMA Official Study System 73
Theory Revision Questions 77
Theory Revision Solutions 78

8 Information Systems and Systems Development 83
Theory Highlights from CIMA Official Study System 85
Theory Revision Questions 89
Theory Revision Solutions 90

9 Information Systems Control and Auditing 95
Theory Highlights from CIMA Official Study System 97
Theory Revision Questions 99
Theory Revision Solutions 100

10 Fraud 103
Theory Highlights from CIMA Official Study System 105
Theory Revision Questions 107
Theory Revision Solutions 108

11 Introduction to Risk Management and Derivatives 113
Theory Highlights from CIMA Official Study System 115
Theory Revision Questions 117
Theory Revision Solutions 119

12 Interest Rate Management 123
Theory Highlights from CIMA Official Study System 125
Theory Revision Questions 127
Theory Revision Solutions 129

13 Foreign Exchange: Relationships and Risks 131
Theory Highlights from CIMA Official Study System 133
Theory Revision Questions 135
Theory Revision Solutions 136

14 Foreign Exchange Risk Management 139
Theory Highlights from CIMA Official Study System 141
Theory Revision Questions 143
Theory Revision Solutions 145

Section 2: Topic – Oriented Exam Questions and Answers with Approach Suggestions 149

Section 3: Comprehensive Exam Questions and Answers with Approach Suggestions 207

Exam Q & As 233

How To Use This Kit

This Practice Kit is an extension of the Learning System authored by Paul M. Collier and Sam Agyei-Ampomah. The theory dealt with in the above-mentioned Learning System is set to revision questions and answers in this Practice Kit. Two new sections have been added. They comprise past exam questions and additional practice questions for the purposes of practicing specifically for the exam. Procedure recommendations are appended, where appropriate, to guide you to prepare your solution that will meet examiner expectations. Where further explanation of a solution is warranted or section of theory in the Learning System is relevant, I have included the explanation or reference in the body of the text adjacent to the guidance icon.

The Learning System Takes Precedence

Every set of questions is preceded by reference to the related theory and highlights the key learning in each section. You are advised to study the entire content of each chapter of the Learning System so that you are adequately prepared to answer questions from the prescribed material. This Practice Kit is intended to aid your preparation for the exam and does not replace the Learning System, change it or limit the examinable content.

Guidance

The approach taken in this practice kit is to provide theory revision questions in Section 1 and then guidance with answering actual exam questions in Sections 2 and 3. Where you see the icons below you will find:

   The author's suggested approach or advice for you to follow.

   Critical learning to be memorised.

Syllabus Guidance, Learning Objectives and Verbs

A The syllabus

The syllabus for the CIMA Professional Chartered Management Accounting qualification 2010 comprises three learning pillars:

- Enterprise Pillar
- Performance Pillar
- Financial Pillar

Within each learning pillar there are three syllabus subjects. Two of these subjects are set at the lower 'Managerial' level, with the third subject positioned at the higher 'Strategic' level. All subject examinations have a duration of 3 hours and the pass mark is 50%.

Note: In addition to these 9 examinations, students are required to gain 3 years relevant practical experience and successfully sit the Test of Professional Competence in Management Accounting (TOPCIMA).

B Aims of the syllabus

The aims of the syllabus are

- to provide for the Institute, together with the practical experience requirements, an adequate basis for assuring society that those admitted to membership are competent to act as management accountants for entities, whether in manufacturing, commercial or service organisations, in the public or private sectors of the economy;
- to enable the Institute to examine whether prospective members have an adequate knowledge, understanding and mastery of the stated body of knowledge and skills;
- to complement the Institute's practical experience and skills development requirements.

C Study weightings

A percentage weighting is shown against each topic in the syllabus. This is intended as a guide to the proportion of study time each topic requires.

All topics in the syllabus must be studied, since any single examination question may examine more than one topic, or carry a higher proportion of marks than the percentage study time suggested.

The weightings *do not* specify the number of marks that will be allocated to topics in the examination.

D Learning outcomes

Each topic within the syllabus contains a list of learning outcomes, which should be read in conjunction with the knowledge content for the syllabus. A learning outcome has two main purposes:

1   to define the skill or ability that a well-prepared candidate should be able to exhibit in the examination;
2   to demonstrate the approach likely to be taken by examiners in examination questions.

The learning outcomes are part of a hierarchy of learning objectives. The verbs used at the beginning of each learning outcome relate to a specific learning objective, for example, evaluate alternative approaches to budgeting.

The verb 'evaluate' indicates a high-level learning objective. As learning objectives are hierarchical, it is expected that at this level, students will have knowledge of different budgeting systems and methodologies and be able to apply them.

A list of the learning objectives and the verbs that appear in the syllabus, learning outcomes and examinations follows:

Learning objectives	Verbs used	Definition
1 Knowledge		
What you are expected to know	List	Make a list of
	State	Express, fully or clearly, the details of/facts of
	Define	Give the exact meaning of
2 Comprehension		
What you are expected to understand	Describe	Communicate the key features of
	Distinguish	Highlight the differences between
	Explain	Make clear or intelligible/State the meaning of
	Identify	Recognise, establish or select after consideration
	Illustrate	Use an example to describe or explain something

3 Application

How you are expected to apply your knowledge

Apply	To put to practical use
Calculate/compute	To ascertain or reckon mathematically
Demonstrate	To prove with certainty or to by practical means
Prepare	To make or get ready for use
Reconcile	To make or prove consistent/compatible
Solve	Find an answer to
Tabulate	Arrange in a table

4 Analysis

How you are expected to analyse the detail of what you have learned

Analyse	Examine in detail the structure of
Categorise	Place into a defined class or division
Compare and contrast	Show the similarities and/or differences between
Construct	To build up or compile
Discuss	To examine in detail by argument
Interpret	To translate into intelligible or familiar terms
Produce	To create or bring into existence

5 Evaluation

How you are expected to use your learning to evaluate, make decisions or recommendations

Advise	To counsel, inform or notify
Evaluate	To appraise or assess the value of
Recommend	To advise on a course of action

Learning Outcomes, Syllabus Content and Examination Format

Paper P3 – Performance Strategy

Syllabus outline

The syllabus comprises:

Topic and study weighting

- A   Management Control Systems   10%
- B   Risk and Internal Control   25%
- C   Review and Audit of Control Systems 15%
- D   Management of Financial Risk   35%
- E   Risk and Control in Information Systems 15%

 Sections B and D have been substantially upgraded in terms of their weighting and future exams will be reflective of these changes. In particular, the weighting of the management of financial risk has now been increased to over a third of the paper and participants are advised to prepare more comprehensively in this regard. You are strongly advised to augment your studies with the recommended reading as suggested by the authors of the official CIMA *Learning System*.

Learning aims

Students should be able to

- evaluate and advise on management and internal control systems for a range of risks;
- plan a review process, including an internal audit, of such systems;
- evaluate alternatives and advise on the management of financial risks;
- advise on the development of information systems that support the risk control environment.

Assessment Strategy

There will be a written examination paper of 3 hours, plus 20 minutes of pre-examination question paper reading time. The examination paper will have the following sections:

Section A – 50 marks
A maximum of four compulsory questions, totalling 50 marks, all relating to a pre-seen case study and further new unseen case material provided within the examination. (Note: The pre-seen case study is common to all three of the Strategic level papers at each examination sitting i.e. paper E3, P3 and F3.)

Section B – 50 marks
Two questions, from a choice of three, each worth 25 marks. Short scenarios will be given, to which some or all questions relate.

Learning Outcomes and Indicative Syllabus Content

P3 – A. Management Control Systems (10%)

Learning Outcomes		Indicative Syllabus Content
Lead	Component	
1. Evaluate control systems for organisational activities and resources. (5)	(a) Evaluate and recommend appropriate control systems for the management of an organisation. (b) Evaluate the appropriateness of an organisation's management accounting control systems. (c) Evaluate the control of activities and resources within an organisation. (d) Recommend ways in which identified weaknesses or problems associated with control systems can be avoided or solved.	• The ways in which systems are used to achieve control within the framework of the an organisation (e.g. contracts of employment, policies and procedures, discipline and reward, reporting structures, performance appraisal and feedback). (A–D) • The application of control systems and related theory to the design of management accounting control systems and information systems in general (i.e. control system components, primary and secondary feedback, positive and negative feedback, open- and closed-loop control). (A–D) • Structure and operation of management accounting control systems (e.g. identification of appropriate responsibility and control centres within the organisation, performance target setting, avoiding unintended behavioural consequences of using management accounting controls). (A–D) • Variation in control needs and systems dependent on organisational structure (e.g. extent of centralisation versus divisionalisation, management through strategic business units). (A–D) • Assessing how lean the management accounting system is (e.g. extent of the need for detailed costing, overhead allocation and budgeting, identification of non-value adding activities in the accounting function). (A–D) • Cost of quality applied to the management accounting function and "getting things right first time". (A–D)

P3 – B. Risk and Internal Control (25%)

Learning Outcomes		Indicative Syllabus Content
Lead	**Component**	
1. Identify and discuss evaluate types of risk facing an organisation. (5)	Identify risks facing an organisation: (a) discuss ways of identifying, measuring and assessing the types of risk facing an organisation, including the organisation's ability to bear such risks. (b) produce a report on evaluate risks facing an organisation, including appropriate representations of risk exposure (e.g. a risk map).	• Types and sources of risk for business organisations: financial, commodity price, business (e.g. from fraud, employee malfeasance, litigation, contractual inadequacy, loss of product reputation), technological, external (e.g. economic and political), and corporate reputation (e.g. from environmental and social performance or health and safety) risks. (A) • Fraud related to sources of finance (e.g. advance fee fraud and pyramid schemes). (A) • Risks associated with international operations (e.g. from cultural variations and litigation risk, to loss of goods in transit and enhanced credit risk). (Note: No specific real country will be tested). (A) • Quantification of risk exposures (impact if an adverse event occurs) and their expected values, taking account of likelihood. (A) • Information required to fully report on risk exposures. (B) • Risk map representation of risk exposures as a basis for reporting and analysing risks. (B)

Learning Outcomes

Lead	Component	Indicative Syllabus Content
2. Discuss and evaluate risk management strategies and internal controls. (5)	(a) Discuss the purposes and importance of internal control and risk management for an organisation. (b) Evaluate risk management strategies. (c) Evaluate the essential features of internal control systems for identifying, assessing and managing risks. (d) Evaluate the costs and benefits of a particular internal control system.	• Purposes and importance of internal control and risk management for an organisation. (A) • Issues to be addressed in defining management's risk policy. (B) • The principle of diversifying risk. (Note: Numerical questions will not be set.) (B) • Minimising the risk of fraud (e.g. fraud policy statements, effective recruitment policies and good internal controls, such as approval procedures and separation of functions, especially over procurement and cash). (B, C) • The risk manager role (including as part of a set of roles) as distinct from that of internal auditor. (C) • Purposes of internal control (e.g. safeguarding of shareholders' investment and company assets, facilitation of operational effectiveness and efficiency, contribution to the reliability of reporting). (C) • Elements in internal control systems (e.g. control activities, information and communication processes, processes for ensuring continued effectiveness, etc.). (C) • Operational features of internal control systems (e.g. embedding in company's operations, responsiveness to evolving risks, timely reporting to management). (C) • The pervasive nature of internal control and the need for employee training. (C) • Costs and benefits of maintaining the internal control system. (D)

Learning Outcomes

Lead	Component	Indicative Syllabus Content
3. Discuss and evaluate governance and ethical issues facing an organisation. (5)	(a) Discuss the principles of good corporate governance, particularly as regards the need for internal controls. (b) Evaluate ethical issues as a source of risk to the organisation and recommend control mechanisms for their detection and resolution.	• The principles of good corporate governance based on those for listed companies (the Combined Code), e.g. separation of chairman and CEO roles, appointment of non-executive directors, transparency of directors' remuneration policy, relations with shareholders, the audit committee. Other examples of recommended good practice may include The King Report on Corporate Governance for South Africa, Sarbanes-Oxley Act in the USA, The Smith and Higgs Reports in the UK, etc). (A) • Recommendations for internal control (e.g. The Turnbull Report). (A) • Ethical issues identified in the CIMA Code of Ethics for Professional Accountants, mechanisms for detection in practice and supporting compliance. (B)

P3 – C. Review and Audit of Control Systems (15%)

Learning Outcomes		Indicative Syllabus Content
Lead	**Component**	
1. Discuss the importance of management review of controls. (5)	(a) Discuss the importance of management review of controls.	• The process of review (e.g. regular reporting to management on the effectiveness of internal controls over significant risks) and audit of internal controls. • Major tools available to assist with a review and audit process (e.g. audit planning, documenting systems, internal control questionnaires, sampling and testing).
2. Discuss and evaluate the process and purposes of audit in the context of internal control systems, and produce a plan for such an audit. (5)	(a) Discuss and evaluate the process of internal audit and its relationship to other forms of audit. (b) Produce a plan for the audit of various organisational activities including management, accounting and information systems. (c) Analyse problems associated with the audit of activities and systems, and recommend action to avoid or solve problems associated with the audit of activities and systems.	• Role of the internal auditor and relationship of the internal audit to the external audit. (A) • Relationship of internal audit to other forms of audit (e.g. value-for-money audit, management audit, social and environmental audit). (A) • Operation of internal audit, the assessment of audit risk and the process of analytical review, including different types of benchmarking, their use and limitations. (B, C)

Learning Outcomes

Lead	Component	Indicative Syllabus Content
	(d) Recommend action to improve the efficiency, effectiveness and control of activities.	• Particular relevance of the fundamental principles in CIMA's Ethical Guidelines to the conduct of an impartial and effective review of internal controls. (B, C)
	(e) Discuss the relationship between internal and external audit work.	• Detection and investigation of fraud. (B, D)
		• The nature of the external audit and its process, including the implications of internal audit findings for external audit procedures. (E)
3. Discuss and evaluate corporate governance and ethical issues facing an organisation. (5)	(a) Discuss the principles of good corporate governance for listed companies, for conducting reviews of internal controls and reporting on compliance.	• The principles of good corporate governance for listed companies, for the review of the internal control system and reporting on compliance. (A)
	(b) Discuss the importance of exercising ethical principles in conducting and reporting on internal reviews.	• Application of the CIMA Code of Ethics for Professional Accountants to the resolution of ethical conflicts in the context of discoveries made in the course of internal review, especially section 210. (B)

P3 – D. Management of Financial Risk (35%)

Learning Outcomes		Indicative Syllabus Content
Lead	Component	
1. Identify and evaluate financial risks facing an organisation. (5)	Identify financial risks facing an organisation: (a) evaluate financial risks facing an organisation.	• Sources of financial risk, including those associated with international operations (e.g. hedging of foreign investment value) and trading (e.g. purchase prices and sales values). (A) • Transaction, translation, economic and political risk. (A) • Quantification of risk exposures, their sensitivities to changes in external conditions and their expected values. (A)
2. Identify and evaluate alternative risk management tools. (5)	(a) Identify and evaluate appropriate methods for managing financial risks. (b) Evaluate the effects of alternative methods of risk management and make recommendations accordingly. (c) Explain and discuss exchange rate theory and demonstrate the impact of differential inflation rates on forecast exchange rates. (d) Recommend risk management strategies and discuss their accounting implications.	• Minimising political risk (e.g. gaining government funding, joint ventures, obtaining local finance). (A) • Operation and features of the more common instruments for managing interest rate risk: swaps, forward rate agreements, futures and options. (Note: Numerical questions will not be set involving FRA's, futures or options. See the note below relating to the Black Scholes model.) (A, B, D) • Operation and features of the more common instruments for managing currency risk: swaps, forward contracts, money market hedges, futures and options. (Note: The Black Scholes option pricing model will not be tested numerically, however, an understanding of the variables which will influence the value of an option should be appreciated.) (A, B, D) • Illustration and interpretation of Simple graphs depicting cap, collar and floor interest rate options. (B) • Theory and forecasting of exchange rates (e.g. interest rate parity, purchasing power parity and the Fisher effect). (C) • Principles of valuation of financial instruments for management and financial reporting purposes (IAS 39), and controls to ensure that the appropriate accounting method is applied to a given instrument. (D) • Quantification and disclosure of the sensitivity of financial instrument values to changes in external conditions. (D) • Internal hedging techniques (e.g. netting and matching). (D)

P3 – E. Risk and Control in Information Systems (15%)

Learning Outcomes		Indicative Syllabus Content
Lead	**Component**	
1. Evaluate the benefits and risks associated with information-related systems. (5)	(a) Evaluate and advise managers on the development of information management (IM), information systems (IS) and information technology (IT) strategies that support management and internal control requirements.	• The importance and characteristics of information for organisations and the use of cost–benefit analysis to assess its value. (A, B) • The purpose and content of IM, IS and IT strategies, and their role in performance management and internal control. (A, B) • Data collection and IT systems that deliver information to different levels in the organisation (e.g. transaction processing, decision support and executive informative systems). (A, B)
	(b) Identify and evaluate IS/IT systems appropriate to an organisation's needs for operational and control information.	• The potential ways of organising the IT function (e.g. the use of steering committees, support centres for advice and help desk facilities, end-user participation). (B, C, D) • The arguments for and against outsourcing. (B, C, D) • Methods for securing systems and data back-up in case of systems failure and/or data loss. (B, C, D)
	(c) Evaluate benefits and risks in the structuring and organisation of the IS/IT function and its integration with the rest of the business.	• Minimising the risk of computer-based fraud (e.g. access restriction, password protection, access logging and automatic generation of audit trail). (B, C, D) • Risks in IS/IT systems: erroneous input, unauthorised usage, imported virus infection, unlicensed use of software, theft, corruption of software, etc. (B, C, D)
	(d) Evaluate and recommend improvements to the control of IS; information systems.	• Risks and benefits of Internet and Intranet use by an organisation. (B, C, D) • The criteria for selecting outsourcing/facilities management partners and for managing ongoing relationships, service level agreements, discontinuation/change of supplier, hand-over considerations. (C, D)

Learning Outcomes		Indicative Syllabus Content
Lead	Component	
	(e) Evaluate specific problems and opportunities associated with the audit and control of systems which use IT.	• Controls which can be designed into an information system, particularly one using information technology IT (e.g. security, integrity and contingency controls). (D) • Control and audit of systems development and implementation. (E) • Techniques available to assist audit in a computerised environment (computer-assisted audit techniques e.g. audit interrogation software). (E)

Examination Techniques

Essay questions

Your essay should have a clear structure, that is, an introduction, a middle and an end. Think in terms of 1 mark for each relevant point made. Be careful to include only relevant material because the inclusion of irrelevant content suggests to the examiner that you do not understand the question fully.

Numerical questions

It is essential to show workings in your answer. If you come up with the wrong answer and no workings, the examiner cannot award any marks. However, if you get the wrong answer but apply the correct technique then you will be given some marks.

Reports and memorandum

Where you are asked to produce an answer in a report type format you will be given easy marks for style and presentation.

- A *report* is a document from an individual or group in one organisation sent to an individual or group in another.
- A *memorandum* is an informal report going from one individual or group to another individual or group in the same organisation.

You should start a report as follows:

To: J. SMITH, CEO, ABC plc

From: M ACCOUNTANT

Date: 31 December 20XX

Terms of Reference: Financial Strategy of ABC plc.

The structure of a report is important. It should contain an Introduction which briefly outlines the purpose of the report. Each question or issue should be addressed separately, with appropriate headings. There should also be a conclusion and the report should be signed (not with your real name).

Formulae

Annuity

Present value of an annuity of £1 per annum receivable or payable for n years, commencing in one year, discounted at r% per annum:

$$PV = \frac{1}{r}\left[1 - \frac{1}{[1+r]^n}\right]$$

Perpetuity

Present value of £1 per annum, payable or receivable in perpetuity, commencing in one year, discounted at r% per annum:

$$PV = \frac{1}{r}$$

Growing Perpetuity

Present value of £1 per annum, receivable or payable, commencing in one year, growing in perpetuity at a constant rate of g% per annum, discounted at r% per annum:

$$PV = \frac{1}{r-g}$$

Section 1
Theory Revision

Introduction to Risk and Control

Introduction to Risk and Control

1

LEARNING OUTCOMES

After completing this chapter in the CIMA *Learning System* you should be able to

- understand the inter-relationship between the elements of the *Risk and Control Strategy* syllabus;
- have a broad appreciation of control, governance and risk management;
- appreciate the contribution of audit to risk management and control;
- understand how information systems, fraud, and interest and foreign exchange risk are particular examples of control, governance and risk management that are emphasised in the *Risk and Control Strategy* syllabus.

1.1 Introduction

The main purpose of this chapter is to help candidates see Risk and Control as an integrated subject. The syllabus has five separate elements, each with its own learning outcomes and syllabus content. The key to learning this module is to understand how risk and control are related and how the various elements inter-relate.

The Module map below demonstrates how risk management, informed by management control theory, is carried out in organisations to control the differing categories of risk. Internal controls, accounting controls and IT system controls are discussed and their related audit systems are explored relative to meeting organisational objectives through the process of corporate governance regulation that guides senior management behaviour. Interest rates, derivatives and foreign exchange risks are presented with a view to exploring a range of external controls available to organisations.

1.2 The emergence of risk, governance and control

Risk management has evolved from three separate functional areas: occupational health and safety; insurance; and hedging of financial risks (foreign exchange and interest rates).

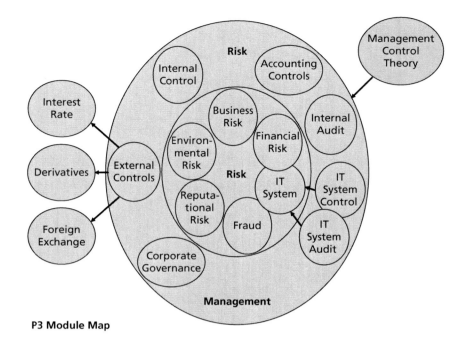

P3 Module Map

The CIMA *Learning System* deals with the impact of these developments and discusses the following areas:

➤ ISO9000
➤ Basel Committee on Banking Supervision (1994)
➤ Value-at-Risk was developed in 1993

The CIMA *Learning System* deals with:

➤ UK Combined Code on Corporate Governance (Financial Reporting Council, 2003)
➤ US the Treadway Commission produced Internal Control – Integrated Framework (COSO, 1992)
➤ US Sarbanes-Oxley Act (SOX) in 2002.

1.3 Corporate governance?

The CIMA *Learning System* discusses the CIMA produced a model of enterprise governance (Chartered Institute of Management Accountants and International Federation of Accountants, 2004) that emphasises the importance of the two dimensions of conformance and performance. Conformance is about satisfying good governance, whilst performance focusses on strategy to improve shareholder value.

1.4 Risk management?

Risk management is the process of understanding and managing risks that the organisation faces in attempting to achieve its objectives. This is a central topic for this module and requires detailed study.

The authors of the CIMA Learning System stress that, while there are different models for risk management (discussed in detail in Chapter 5 of the CIMA *Learning System*), the following seven-step process contains the essential ingredients:

1 Identify the risk
2 Assess the risk impact
3 Risk mapping
4 Record risks in a risk register
5 Risk evaluation
6 Risk treatment
7 Risk reporting.

1.5 Internal control?

Internal control is the whole system of financial and other controls established to provide reasonable assurance of effective and efficient operation; internal financial control and compliance with regulation.

The authors of the CIMA *Learning System* emphasise that an internal control system comprises five elements:

1 A control environment
2 Risk assessment
3 Control activities
4 Monitoring information and
5 Communication.

1.6 Audit?

The audit committee is a committee of the board of directors, the primary function of which is to review the system of internal control, the external audit process, the work of internal audit and the financial information provided to shareholders. The role of audit is covered in Chapter 7 whilst the audit committee is covered in Chapter 4. The CIMA *Learning System* deals with the Internal Audit (as different from external audit) and the relationship with internal controls and risk management.

1.7 A model of governance, risk and control

The authors of the CIMA Learning System stress the importance of your understanding the links between governance, risk management and internal control and the interaction between the board of directors, the audit committee, external and internal auditors, as this is the foundation of the *Risk and Control Strategy* syllabus.

1.8 Fraud, information systems and financial risk

The CIMA *Learning System* integrates the three specific risks: fraud (Chapter 10); information systems (Chapters 8 and 9) and financial derivatives (interest and exchange rate risks, covered in Chapters 11–14) into the core focus of risk management in the *Risk and Control Strategy* syllabus. Information systems risk comprises 20% of the syllabus and financial risk 30% stressing the importance of these sections.

Management Control
Theory

Management Control Theory

2

Theory Highlights from CIMA Official Study System

2.1 Organisations are 'social' because they comprise people. They differ from collectives such as families and social groups in that they are goal-oriented and formalised.

2.2 Organisations are characterised as being cybernetic systems based. Cybernetic systems are self-regulating using a feedback mechanism. Systems can be configured into a complex hierarchy of sub-systems.

2.3 Systems can be either open or closed. Closed systems are isolated from the environment meaning that they cannot be changed or influenced. Open systems are influenced by the environment and can be changed. Organisations are configured as open systems facilitating control by management.

2.4 Organisations, as cybernetic systems, contain three levels namely: target-setting level, operations level and control level.

    2.4.1 Typical targets for business are EVA™, ROI and ROCE and these targets which we use will be really reflected in budgets and standard costs.

    2.4.2 Operations is concerned with converting inputs into outputs.

    2.4.3 Control is carried out through a system in which there is provision for corrective action through either a feedback or a feedforward mechanism.

2.5 There are five major standards against which performance can be compared: previous time periods, similar organisations, estimates of future organisational performance *ex ante*, estimates of what might have been achieved *ex post* and the performance necessary to achieve defined goals.

2.6 In this module, we are concerned with selected theories of management and control. The following are key definitions (CIMA *Official Terminology*):

    2.6.1 **Control:** The ability to direct the financial and operating policies of an entity with a view to obtaining economic benefits from its activities.

    2.6.2 **Management control:** All of the processes used by managers to ensure that organisational goals are achieved and procedures adhered to, and that the organisation responds appropriately to changes in its environment.

    2.6.3 **Control environment:** The overall attitude, awareness and actions of directors and management regarding internal controls and their importance to the entity . . . [it] encompasses the management style, and corporate culture and values shared by all employees. It provides a background against which the various other controls are operated.

    2.6.4 **Control procedures:** Those policies and procedures in addition to their control environment which are established to achieve that entity's specific objectives.

2.7 Anthony's (1965) classic categorisation of control was at three levels: strategic, management and operational. His work highlighted the interface between strategic planning and operational control such that management control ensured that day-to-day operations were consistent with the overall strategy.

2.8 Otley and Berry (1980) defined management control as monitoring activities and then taking action to ensure that desired ends are attained. (See Figure 1.2 in the *Learning System*).

2.9 Central to the cybernetic process is learning. Systems having feedback mechanisms will derive little benefit if learning was not taken place. Fiol and Lyles (1985) defined organisation learning as: "The development of insights, knowledge, and associations between past actions, the effectiveness of those actions, and future actions." They contrasted adaptation, through incremental change, to the environment to other changes. For all purposes, these changes will require creative action (as described by Ford and Ogilvie, 1996) in order to bring about the creation of new knowledge and competitive advantage. (See Figure 1.3 in the *Learning System*).

2.10 It is important to understand the differences in typology for management control (Hofstede, 1981). They are divided into two main groups: cybernetic and non-cybernetic. Cybernetic management controls have feedback mechanisms that enable learning and adjustment to the organisational system so that future actions will be different from past actions. Non-cybernetic controls lack feedback mechanisms meaning that these controls relate to specific operations and the organisational system cannot benefit from learning because there is no feedback mechanism.

2.11 Management styles can be defined in many different ways. One such grouping comprises:

    2.11.1 Autocratic – a style of management where the com monde structure is required to be obeyed at all times. The military is organized along these lines.

    2.11.2 Paternalistic – a dictatorial style of management where commands are required to be obeyed but where the management tend to make decisions in the best interests of the employee.

    2.11.3 Democratic – a consultative style of management where the opinion and input of the employee is encouraged in the process of decision-making.

2.11.4 Laissez-faire – a hands-off style of management where highly skilled employees are empowered to make their own decisions with little or no direction from superiors.

2.12 Four main organisational structure types are discussed namely: functional structure; divisionalised structure, matrix structures and network structure. Structure is dependent upon the strategy of the organisation. Functional structures are associated with centralised hierarchical organisations; divisionalised structures with multi-national and flat-structured organisations; matrix structures are associated with multi-national or broadly geographically spread organisations but also with project team-oriented organisations; network structures are associated with organisations where collaboration or pooling of resources deliver synergistic advantages.

2.13 Three main responsibilities centre types are: cost centres, profit centres and investment centres.

2.13.1 **Financial control in divisionalised businesses is defined as:** the control of divisional performance by setting a range of targets and monitoring of actual performance towards these targets.

Theory Revision Questions

The questions in this section are intended to assist you with learning the relevant concepts relating to management control theory. It is important to memorise and learn these concepts and tools for later recall in the examination. After studying this section, you should attempt the questions in Sections 2 and 3. Questions in sections 2 and 3 enable you to apply these concepts and tools in composite business problem scenarios. The examination is designed around composite scenario problem solving type questions and Sections 2 and 3 have informed mainly on past exam papers as examples for you to prepare appropriately.

2.1 What characteristics distinguish organisations from other collectives such as families and social groups?

2.2 Why would organisations be described as *social?*

2.3 Describe a Cybernetic System.

2.4 Differentiate between an open and a closed system.

2.5 Discuss the three levels of an organisation as a cybernetic system.

2.6 Is control limited to financial control?

2.7 Distinguish between automated and manual controls and provide suitable examples.

2.8 Differentiate between FEEDFORWARD and FEEDBACK.

2.9 Name the FIVE standards for control.

2.10 Define *control.*

2.11 Define *management control.*

2.12 Define *control environment.*

2.13 Define *control procedures.*

2.14 Discuss Anthony's (1965) classic categorisation of control.

2.15 Name the four conditions of the Otley & Berry management control model.

2.16 What are the limitations of the Otley & Berry management control model?

2.17 Define organisational learning in terms of Fiol & Lyles (1985).

2.18 Why is it creative action important to organisations?

2.19 Describe and contrast the various control types comprising Hofstede's (1981) typology for management control.

2.20 Give two examples of each of the control types in Hofstede's typology.

2.21 Differentiate between the Functional and Divisional structure forms.

2.22 Describe the Matrix structure for an organisation and give two examples.

2.23 Where would a Network structure be appropriate for an organisation?

2.24 Name three forms of responsibility centre and describe their major benefits and limitations.

2.25 What are the most common measures for profit and investment centres and why are they considered to be the most appropriate measure?

2.26 Define and discuss controllability as it relates to the divisionalised organisation.

☑ Theory Revision Solutions

2.1 Goal-orientation and formalisation are two characteristics that distinguish organisations from other collectives such as families and social groups.

2.2 Organisations can be described as social because they comprise people.

2.3 A cybernetic system is a system that has a self-regulating feedback mechanism. It can comprise a complex hierarchy of sub-systems.

2.4 An open system can be influenced by the environment while a closed system is independent from the influences of the environment.

2.5 *Target-setting:* The performance standards and targets set for the organisation; *Operations:* The process of converting inputs to outputs that meet market demands; *Control:* Comparison of actual performance with targets.

2.6 Control is not limited to financial control but includes operational and other forms of control (over behaviour, quality, recruitment, etc.)

2.7 Automated control systems are those systems that are programmed into hardware and software technology-based solutions. Examples include building access controls, event alerts such as payments exceeding a stated value and engineering solutions like vault door timed delays, etc.. Manual controls include:

   (a) Authority and responsibility structuring. The reporting lines and organisational management structure are examples of organisational structuring which has a profound impact upon the style and process of management.
   (b) Policies and procedures governing the methods of operating within the organisation. Best known of all are the accounting policies and procedures which govern the basic points of departure, methodologies, processes and outputs required.
   (c) Rewards and discipline governing targets, behaviour and performance of individuals and groups. Contemporary infamous examples are the bonuses paid to investment bankers for short-term performance that ultimately resulted in long-term organisational failure.
   (d) Performance appraisal and feedback directing goal objectives for individuals. Examples include 360° peer review appraisals and Balanced Scorecard™ based quantitative and qualitative assessments.

2.8 *Feedforward* control is the process of forecasting differences between actual and planned outcomes, and implementation of action, before the event, to avoid such differences (CIMA *Official Terminology*). *Feedback* control is the measurement of differences between planned outputs and actual outputs achieved, and the modification of subsequent action and/or plans to achieve future required results (CIMA *Official Terminology*).

2.9 1 Previous time periods
     2 Similar organisations
     3 *Exante* – estimates of future performance
     4 *Expost* – estimates of what might have been achieved
     5 The performance necessary to achieve defined goals.

2.10 *Control:* The ability to direct the financial and operationg policies of an entity with a view to gaining economic benefits from its activities (CIMA *Official Terminology*).

2.11 *Management control:* All of the processes used by managers to ensure that organisational goals are achieved and procedures adhered to, and that the organisation responds appropriately to changes in its environment (CIMA *Official Terminology*).

2.12 *Control environment:* The overall attitude, awareness and actions of directors and management regarding internal controls and their importance to the entity . . . [it] encompasses the management style, and corporate culture and values shared by all employees. It provides a background against which the various other controls are operated.

2.13 *Control procedures:* Those policies and procedures in addition to the control environment which are established to achieve the entity's specific objectives.

2.14 Anthony's classic categorisation has three levels:

1 *Strategic control:* Comprising strategic planning, governance procedures, determining the organisation's structure, corporate policies and monitoring. Domain of the Board and CEO.
2 *Management control:* Concerned with implementing strategy and procedures and monitoring performance to ensure it is consistent with strategy and achieves performance targets. Domain of Middle Management.
3 *Operational control:* Takes place at the task level of day-to-day activity where structured and repetitive activities take place. Domain of first-line supervisors.

2.15 1 The existence of an objective that is desired;
2 A means of measuring process outputs in terms of this objective;
3 The ability to predict the effect of potential control actions; and
4 The ability to take actions to reduce deviations from the objective.

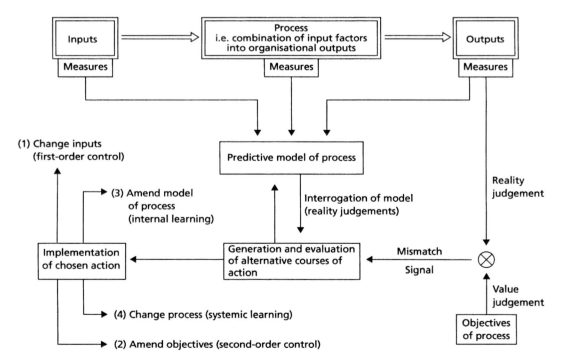

Figure Outline scheme of necessary conditions for a controlled process (Reprinted from Accounting, Organizations and Society, Vol. 5, No. 2, D.T. Otley & A.J. Berry, Control, organization and accounting, pp. 231–44, Copyright 1980, Elsevier Science)

These conditions conform to the concept of a cybernetic control process. The Inputs > Process > Outputs model is extended to include a predictive model of the process. This describes the cause – effect relationships that management believe to be true about how resources (inputs) are converted (process) into results (outputs). Results may be financial but may also be concerned with product quality, customer satisfaction, market share, employee motivation, etc.

2.16 According to Otley & Berry (1980), some factors that the model does not cater for are:

(a) Organisational objectives are often vague and ambiguous [unclear]. . . . measures of achievement are possible only in correspondingly vague and often subjective terms …

If objectives are unclear and stated in terms that limit objective measurement then clear and accurate feedback will be limited making corrective action difficult;

(b) Change with time.

The effect of this is to make prediction more difficult and increases the risks – something we deal with in greater detail in Chapter 3;

(c) Different models are held by different participants.

The effectiveness of a team is dependant upon the cohesiveness of the participants and if they have differing objectives then the processes will produce differing outputs.

2.17 Fiol & Lyles (1985) define organisational learning as "The development of insights, knowledge, and associations between past actions, the effectiveness of those actions, and future actions."

In order to adapt to changes in the environment, the organisation must be able to detect and monitor changes in the environment and adapt (or learn) to deal with those changes. It is therefore critical that organisations understand human learning processes so that they can structure their organisations and processes to accommodate human learning to ensure that they survive and can capitalise on strategic opportunities. Learning includes gaining a better understanding of the resources required, the predictive model (see 1.14 above), and how to measure outputs.

2.18 Creative actions are those actions that bring about something new (new knowledge) that enable the management to act or react to the changing environment. " . . and the lessons learned from taking action are an indispensable source of knowledge creation and competitive advantage." (Extract from Ford & Ogilvie, 1996, p. 58)

2.19 Hofstede (1981) developed a management control typology. Six types were identified of which three are cybernetic in nature [because learning takes place or feedback can be deployed to influence the control system] and the remaining three not.

Cybernetic controls:
Routine control takes place where there are clearly defined objectives, the outputs are measurable, there are known effects of the intervention and the activity is repetitive.

Expert control takes place where objectives are ambiguous, outputs measurable, effects of intervention known but activity is non-repetitive.

Trial-and-error control takes place in an environment where objectives are unambiguous, outputs measurable but effects of interventions *not* known and the control is repetitive.

Non-cybernetic controls:
Intuitive controls take place where objectives are unambiguous, outputs measurable but effects of interventions *not* known and where activity is non-repetitive.

Judgemental controls take place where objectives are unambiguous, outputs are *not* measurable, effects of interventions are *not* known and are non-repetitive.

Political control takes place where the objectives are ambiguous, outputs are *not* measurable, effects of interventions *not* known and control is non-repetitive.

A method for remembering the typology is to construct the following table:

Control Type	Objectives	Outputs	Effects of Interventions	Activity
Cybernetic				
Routine	Unambiguous	Measurable	Known	Repetitive
Expert	Ambiguous	Measurable	Known	Non-repetitive
Trial-and-error	Unambiguous	Measurable	Not known	Repetitive
Non-cybernetic				
Intuitive	Unambiguous	Measurable	Not known	Non-repetitive
Judgemental	Unambiguous	Not measurable	Not known	Non-repetitive
Political	Ambiguous	Not measurable	Not known	Non-repetitive

For a control to meet the requirements to be classified as cybernetic, learning must take place within the organisation.

2.20   You were required to give *two* examples. I have provided a few more.

Routine: Banking, letter posting, supermarket checkout, filing, bookkeeping, flight check-in. Control is through predetermined rules and routines.

Expert: Engineering design, medical operation, accounting audit. Control is through an external expert with prior knowledge of the processes.

Trial-and-error: New product launch, launching a prototype rocket, freeing rehabilitated wildlife, sampling an ore body for gold. Control is through learning from failure, through ex-post analysis of the event.

Intuitive: Leading a demoralised football club, selecting staff. Control is an art rather than a science.

Judgemental: A social welfare initiative, a concession to a staff member, resolution of a conflict between two or more parties. Control becomes a matter of subjective judgement.

Political: Public sector organisations, meeting the demands of an influential shareholder, towing the company line. Control is dependant upon power relationships.

2.21 Functional structure is typified by the hierarchy where decision-making is located at the top of the hierarchy and activities grouped according to function (e.g. marketing, finance, production, distribution). Each department executes the functions for all other departments.

Divisional structure is typified by decentralised decision-making devolved to groups based upon major business elements (e.g. Country offices, product line specialists, customer profile groups). Each division has its own functions.

2.22 The matrix structure is a combination of the functional and the divisional structure. Here, the control is shared by the functional manager and the divisional manager.

Examples include control of a sales force in multiple countries. The staff reports to the divisional (country) manager in respect of daily discipline and to the International product manager in respect of the product sales.

2.23 Network structures are best suited to partnerships or collaborations of organizations with different ownerships and objectives exploiting synergy for specialised skill and knowledge. Examples include outsourcing of services or collaborative logistics handling between a client and their supplier.

> In the globalised context it is important to note that international industry associations, international regulatory authorities, recognised international standards and customer associations are becoming increasingly important in the corporate network.

2.24 The three forms of responsibility centre are:

1 Cost centres
2 Profit centres
3 Investment centres.

2.25 The most common accounting measures of divisional performance are:

- Return on investment (ROI) for profit centres; and
- Residual income (RI) for investment centres.

2.26 Merchant (1987) describes the principle of controllability where individuals are only held accountable for the results that they can control. This highlights one of the limitations of operating profit as a measure of divisional performance. It includes costs over which the divisional manager has no control. When divisions trade within the same group, conflicts arise between the requirement for the group as a whole to make a profit and the profit maximisation objectives of each particular division. Internal transfer pricing policy can favour or prejudice particular divisions.

Further, objectives and interpretation of performance evaluation between head office and the division will often be quite different and this may result in manipulating of the accounting reports to favour performance measurement of objectives.

Accounting Control and Behavioural Consequences

Accounting Control and Behavioural Consequences

3

LEARNING OUTCOMES

After completing this chapter in the CIMA *Learning System* you should be able to

- evaluate and recommend appropriate control systems for the management of organisations;
- evaluate the control of activities and resources within the organisation;
- recommend ways in which the problems associated with control systems can be avoided or solved;
- evaluate the appropriateness of an organisation's management accounting control systems and make recommendations for improvements.

Theory Highlights from CIMA Official Study System

3.1 This section discusses the intended and unintended behavioural consequences of quantitative and qualitative measurement methodologies.

3.2 Standard costing, capital investment appraisal, transfer pricing, budget variance analysis and overhead allocation techniques that make up the traditional measurement methodologies offer the user stability and simplicity on the one hand, but constrained by potential over-simplification and broad approximation leading to the risk of inappropriate decisions on the other. Enhancements, notably activity based costing (ABC), flexed budgets and the addition of strategic cost accounting has extended the use of these instruments to more modern methodologies. Even with these modern advances, indirect cost allocation remains, to a somewhat lesser degree, an approximation.

3.3 Inter-departmental/SBU pricing policies (transfer pricing) remains a contentious issue. Transfer prices that are used for measuring business unit success and rewarding managers of business units can be counterproductive for the overall good of the greater organisation. Globalisation is compounding the problem and, with the intervention of governments in respect of counter-tax management strategies, organisations are faced with governance, risk and operational challenges.

3.4 Budgeting has had a long and fruitful role to play in the process of organisational control. However, human behaviour being what it is, in many organisations power, political posturing and gaming take precedence over objective and accurate budgeting linked to strategic objectives. Organisations like the Beyond Budgeting Round Table argue that budgeting is counterproductive, provides poor value to users, fails to focus on shareholder value, is too rigid and stifles response, protects rather than reduces costs, stifles product and strategy innovation, focuses inappropriately on sales targets rather than customer satisfaction and is often divorced from strategy.

3.5 As with many other aspects of risk management, budgets tend to reinforce a dependency culture that can lead to unethical behaviour or compliance behaviour that exposes the organisation to heightened risk.

3.6 Standard costing provides a platform upon which actual to planned variances can be analysed. With the advent of computerisation, flexed budgets provide a more advanced approach to managing costs and cost variances.

3.7 JIT, TQM, Six Sigma and emergent accounting techniques including strategic management accounting, life-cycle costing, target costing and Kaizen techniques are enhancing the capabilities of organisations' management teams to better manage production, customer-orientated demand with corresponding improvements and rationalisation of accounting (e.g. Backflush accounting used in JIT manufacturing). Lean management accounting eliminates wasteful accounting practices. For example, it does not rely on detailed transaction reporting but uses backflush costing linked to final output rather than at each stage of production.

3.8 The advantages of JIT, Michael Porter's value chain theory and focused attention on value adding activities, has accelerated the acceptance of a lean manufacturing and lean management accounting.

3.9 In all of the deliberations, we need to be conscious of the fact that controls in general, and accounting controls in particular, could lead to dysfunctional behaviour where measurements and demands made on individuals leave room for behaviour that is counter to the best interests of the organisation.

3.10 Non-financial performance measurement systems such as the Balanced Scorecard are increasingly important in supplementing financially based management accounting information.

3.11 It cannot be overemphasised that close attention to the design of quantitative and qualitative measures is necessary to reinforce desired outcomes and control dysfunctional consequences. The management accountant is well placed, as a result of her professional training and skill, to guide and manage risk controls and measurements to bring about positive valued adding outcomes.

Theory Revision Questions

The questions in this section are intended to assist you with learning the relevant concepts relating to accounting control systems. It is important to memorise and learn these concepts and tools for later recall in the examination. After studying this section, you should attempt the questions in Sections 2 and 3. Questions in Sections 2 and 3 enable you to apply these concepts and tools in composite business problem scenarios. The examination is designed around composite scenario problem solving type questions and Sections 2 and 3 have informed mainly on past exam papers as examples for you to prepare appropriately.

3.1   List the main accounting methods through which control is exercised.

3.2   Define *Standard costing*.

3.3   Describe the three main methods of capital investment appraisal.

3.4   What alternative analysis techniques could provide a better fit (other than DCF modelling) between investment decisions and business strategy implementation?

3.5   Explain how activity-based costing improves cost measurement.

3.6   List three purposes of budgeting.

3.7   Describe how feedforward and feedback loops influence budgeting processes.

3.8   Describe three problems in the budgeting process that could influence the validity of a budget as a control mechanism.

3.9   What are the primary difficulties associated with budgeting?

3.10 List the reasons why budgets cause problems according to the Beyond Budgeting Round Table (www.bbrt.co.uk/).

3.11 Discuss the fundamental differences between traditional budgeting and 'beyond budgeting'.

3.12 Describe the role of variance analysis in the budgetary control process.

3.13 How does the Just In Time (JIT) management technique affect the accounting process?

3.14 Why is standard costing seen to be restrictive when TQM techniques are applied?

3.15 Define the cost of quality.

3.16 Describe the two broad categories of cost of quality.

3.17 List four emerging management accounting techniques.

3.18 Identify the characteristics of SMA.

3.19 What are the benefits of life-cycle costing?

3.20 Target costing is concerned with managing whole-of-life costs *during the design phase*. Its aim is to build a product at a cost that could be recovered over the product lifecycle through a price that customers would be willing to pay to obtain the benefits. Describe the stages of target costing that support the above objectives.

3.21 Discuss the difference in focus between Kaizen and target costing in the product life cycle.

3.22 What are the five principles of the lean management accounting?

3.23 Define Backflush costing.

3.24 Identify the dysfunctional consequences of budgeting.

3.25 Describe the unintended consequences of performance measurement.

☑ Theory Revision Solutions

3.1   Control is exercised through the following main accounting methods:

1   Standard costing
2   Capital investment appraisal
3   Overhead allocation
4   Transfer pricing
5   Budgets and budgetary control.

3.2   *Standard costing* is a control technique which compares standard costs and revenues with actual results to obtain variances which are used to stimulate improved performance (CIMA *Official Terminology*)

3.3   The three main methods of capital investment appraisal are:

1   Accounting rate of return which computes the annual cash flows minus depreciation divided by the initial investment.
2   Payback period computes the time period over which the initial investment is returned.
3   Discounted cash flow (DCF) which requires estimation of future incremental cash flows (additional cash flows based on income net of expenses) that will result from the investment, discounted at a rate of return required from the project.

3.4   Shank (1996) argued that a strategic cost management approach could apply value chain analysis, cost driver analysis and competitive advantage analysis to achieve a better fit between investment decisions and business strategy implementation.

   Strategic cost management is an approach that focuses management attention on external factors that influence market parameters and cost of the organisation. Shank's approach argues, from a more practical perspective, that the application of value chain analysis, which provides an insight into the customer value adding aspects of the organisation, cost driver analysis which links cost determination to decision-making on a cause-and-effect basis, and competitive advantage analysis which informs the sustainable strategic advantage, will provide a more reliable measure of value creation than the output from DCF modelling by addressing the 'richness' of the situation. He argues that a strategic cost management approach will form the basis for decision-making based upon known strengths that the organisation is capable of exploiting. Analysis based upon pre-existing resource and skill provides a link between the organisation's pre-existing competitive advantage and proposed investment. This method measures prospective investments in terms of those advantages. By executing DCF modelling, we are evaluating the potential investment independent from the investing organisation. The key question that Shank raises is whether the investment will have a synergistic fit with the investing organisation's competitive advantage.

3.5   Activity-based costing requires that all costs are allocated to the product or products based upon the consumption by the respective products of activities. Costs of activities, that cannot be traced to the products directly, are arranged in cost pools. Each cost pool collects costs based upon the influence of a cost driver that best correlates cause-and-effect for that group of activities. While activity based costing methods are based upon approximation, because of the higher degree of correlation between the cost drivers and the consumption of activities, the degree of inaccuracy is reduced and, thereby improving the quality of information for decision-making.

3.6   The three purposes of budgeting, according to Emmanuel et al. (1990) are:

1   A full cost of future events
2   As motivational targets
3   As standards for performance evaluation.

3.7   Feedforward loops enable managers to review budgets before implementation in order to ensure that the budget reflects the organisation's goals and objectives of the strategies. Feedback loops enable management to measure the difference between actual output and planned output of the organisation.

3.8   Three possible problems that could arise in the budgeting process that could limit its performance in its role as a control mechanism are:

1   *Gaming*: Low targets are set because managers believe these will be readily achieved. This has the effect of reducing budgeting to a process of negotiation rather than detailed planning.
2   *Creative accounting*: Manipulating results so that targets are achieved, particularly where these are linked with performance bonuses.
3   *Achievement motive*: Once targets are achieved, managers may no longer be motivated to continue their efforts, particularly as this may result in higher targets being set in the future.

3.9   The primary difficulties related to budgeting are in predicting the volume of sales for the business, especially the sales mix between different products or services and the timing of income and expenses.

3.10 The list of 10 reasons why budgets cause problems according to the Beyond Budgeting Round Table (www.bbrt.co.uk/) are listed below:

Budgets:

1   Are time-consuming and expensive
2   Provide poor value to users
3   Fail to focus on shareholder value
4   Are too rigid and prevent fast response
5   Protect rather than reduce costs
6   Stifle product and strategy innovations
7   Focus on sales targets rather than customer satisfaction
8   Are divorced from strategy
9   Reinforce a dependency culture
10 Can lead to unethical behavior.

3.11 The two fundamental differences between traditional budgeting and the 'beyond budgeting' models are:

1   The beyond budgeting model is more adaptive. In place of fixed annual plans and budgets that tie managers to predetermined actions, targets are reviewed regularly and based on stretch goals linked to performance against world-class benchmarks and prior periods.
2   The beyond budgeting model enables a more decentralised way of managing. In-place of the traditional hierarchy and centralised leadership, it enables decision-making and performance accountability to be devolved to line managers and creates a self-managed working environment and a culture of personal responsibility.

3.12   Variance analysis involves comparing actual performance against planned, investigating the causes of the variance and taking corrective action to ensure that targets are achieved.

3.13   JIT techniques provide for the reduction in inter-stage manufacturing buffer inventories and reduce cycle times substantially. Work-in-progress inventories are virtually eliminated. These characteristics have the effect of reducing the need for inter-stage accounting due to the minimal amount of inventory in progress at any one time. This has given rise to Backflush costing techniques. Typically, Accounting stages are reduced to raw material, finished goods and cost of goods sold.

3.14   Standard costing techniques can be restrictive when a TQM approach is adopted because there will be a tendency to aim at the more obvious cost reductions (cheaper labour and materials) rather than the aims of TQM which are improvement in quality, reliability, on-time delivery, flexibility, etc.

> An important observation is that budgeting, standard costing and variance analysis should not be deployed without taking the wider array of measurement techniques into account and weighing the outputs from the broader measurement array in the decision-making process.

3.15   The cost of quality is 'the difference between the actual costs of producing, selling and supporting products or services and the equivalent costs if there were no failures during production for usage.' (CIMA *Official Terminology*)

3.16   The two broad categories of cost of quality are:

1   *Conformance costs* which are costs incurred to achieve the specified standard of quality and include prevention costs and costs of appraisal.
2   *Non-conformance* costs are costs which include both internal and external failures.

3.17   Emerging management accounting techniques include:

1   Strategic management accounting
2   Life-cycle costing
3   Target costing
4   Kaizen costing.

3.18   According to Lord (1996), SMA is comprised of:

- The collection of competitor information: pricing, costs, volume and market share;
- Exploitation of cost reduction opportunities: a focus on continuous improvement and on non-financial performance measures;
- Matching the accounting emphasis with the firm's strategic position.

3.19   Life-cycle costing helps to determine whether the profits generated during the production phase cover all the life-cycle costs.

> This is particularly valuable in modern industries where up to 80% of the costs of the product can be incurred during the development phase. With life-cycles for-products substantially reduced, particularly in the technology field, it is important for management to be able to predict future product/service development costs associated with new products and to evaluate market conditions and pricing to ensure that the development costs are recovered over the life cycle of the product.

3.20 Target costing has four stages:

1 Determining the target price which customers will be prepared to pay for the product/service;
2 Deducting a target profit margin to determine the target cost which becomes the cost to which the product/service should be engineered;
3 Estimating the actual cost of the product/service based on the current design;
4 Investigating ways of reducing the estimated cost to the target cost.

3.21 Target costing is a 'before-the-event' process involving the entire products cost evaluation at the design phase. Kaizen costing is applied during the production phase of the life cycle when large innovations may not be possible – hence the name Kaizen (Japanese term for the word 'tightening') where the focus falls on continuous improvement to the production process. The investigation of cost reduction is a cost-to-function analysis that examines the relationship between how much cost is spent on the primary functions of the product/service compared to the secondary functions.

3.22 The five principles of lean management accounting are:

1 *Value provided to customers* is reflected in the price by using a *target costing* approach;
2 *Value stream management*: Managing the business through processes or value streams rather than traditional departmental structures;
3 Flow of products and services through the value stream while *eliminating waste*;
4 *Pull* to enable flow of products and services based on customer demand *rather than push* through production processes;
5 *Perfection* through quality improvement which is both continuous and break-through.

3.23 Backflush costing is a method of costing, associated with a JIT (Just In Time) production system, which applies cost to the output of a process. Costs do not mirror the flow of products through the production process, but are attached to output produced (finished goods stock and cost of sales), on the assumption that such backflushed costs are a realistic measure of the actual cost incurred. (CIMA *Official Terminology*)

3.24 Budgeting dysfunctional behaviour includes:

Smoothing: Shifting revenue or expenses from one accounting period to another to eliminate sharp fluctuations in reported performance.
Biasing: The selection of a message that the recipient wants to hear, such as a high forecast (because that is what is wanted) rather than one perceived to be more realistic.
Focussing: Placing emphasis on certain positive aspects of performance rather than other negative ones.
Gaming: Pursuit of a particular performance standard in response to that demanded of the participant even though they know that this is not in the organisation's best interest in terms of its strategy. The creation of 'slack' (asking for more than what is required) to cushion performance requirements and/or to provide padding to counteract budget reduction practices of senior managers; spending budget allocations at the year end whether the expenditure is needed or not.
Filtering: Data are filtered so that desirable aspects of performance are reported by the information system while undesirable aspects of performance are suppressed.
Illegal acts: An action that violates organisational rules.

3.25   Smith (1995), in a public sector study, found the following eight unintended consequences of performance measurement:

1   *Tunnel vision*: The emphasis on quantifiable data at the expense of qualitative data.
2   *Sub-optimisation*: the pursuit of narrow local objectives at the expense of broader organisation-wide ones.
3   *Myopia*: The short-term focus on performance may have a longer-term consequences.
4   *Measure fixation*: An emphasis on measures rather than the underlying objective.
5   *Misrepresentation*: The deliberate manipulation of data so that reported behaviour is different from actual behaviour.
6   *Gaming*: The pursuit of a particular performance standard in response to that demanded of the participant while knowing that this is not in the organisation's best interest in terms of its strategy.
7   *Ossification*: Performance measurement can inhibit innovation and lead to paralysis of action.
8   *Misinterpretation*: The way in which the performance measure is explained.

Corporate Governance and the Audit Committee

Corporate Governance and the Audit Committee

4

LEARNING OUTCOMES

After completing this chapter in the CIMA *Learning System* you should be able to

- explain the principles of good corporate governance for listed companies (using the UK system as a model), particularly as regards the need for internal controls;
- discuss the principles of good corporate governance for listed companies, for conducting reviews of internal controls and reporting on compliance.

Theory Highlights from CIMA Official Study System

4.1 The rise of corporate governance is largely in response to the spate of corporate failures across the world. Culminating in the *Combined Code*, the UK reporting requirements for FTSE listed companies has developed over the last decade into robust requirements for boards of directors to demonstrate and disclose their compliance with 'best practice' in respect of corporate governance recommendations.

4.2 Corporate governance models are comprised either of shareholder value/agency models or stakeholder models. The UK corporate governance model is premised in the shareholder value/agency model. The South African corporate governance model, by contrast, is an example of a stakeholder model.

4.3 The *Combined Code* places specific responsibilities upon the board of directors with regards to the composition, structure and defined committee activities of the board. Specific committees, comprised mostly of non-executive directors are charged with the responsibility of determining director remuneration, overseeing audit standards and reviewing board nominations.

4.4 Of these committees, the audit committee fulfils a pivotal role in corporate control. Code C3 of the Combined Code states: *the board should establish an audit committee of at least three, or in the case of smaller companies two members, who should all be independent non-executive directors. The board should satisfy itself that at least one member of the audit committee has a recent and relevant financial experience.*

4.5 CIMA defines an audit committee as: *A formally constituted sub-committee of the main board which should normally meet at least twice a year. Membership of the committee should comprise at least three directors, all non-executive. The majority of the committee members should be independent of the company. The primary function of the audit committee is to assist the board to fulfil its stewardship responsibilities by reviewing the systems of internal control, the external audit process, the work of the internal audit and the financial information which is provided to shareholders* (CIMA *Official Terminology*).

4.6 The combined code guidance on audit committees is referred to as the Smith Guidance. The Smith Guidance emphasises that: . . . a frank, open working relationship and a high level of mutual respect are essential, particularly between the audit committee chairman and the board chairman, the chief executive and the finance director. The audit committee must be prepared to take a robust stand, and all parties must be prepared to make information freely available to the audit committee, to listen to their views and to talk through the issues openly (para. 1.7).

4.7 The benefits of good corporate governance include risk reduction, performance stimulation, enhanced access to capital markets, improved customer and supplier perception, leadership enhancement and shareholder confidence. Organisation's recognising the benefits of good corporate governance and stimulating corporate culture towards its acceptance are benefiting from the competitive advantages that it brings through heightened market image and the resultant trust in the organisation by investors.

4.8 Developments within the banking industry, with the advent of the Basel II Accord that is being rolled out internationally at present, brings greater emphasis upon real-time empirical data based credit risk rating and greater emphasis upon operational risk management that is more difficult to assess.

4.9 Corporate governance is the system by which companies are directed and controlled. Boards of directors are responsible for the governance of their companies. The responsibility of the Board includes setting the companies aims, providing the leadership to put those aims into effect, supervising the management of the business and reporting to shareholders on their stewardship (CIMA *Official Terminology*).

4.10 The Audit Committee monitors the integrity of financial statements, reviews the company's internal control and risk management systems, monitors the effectiveness of internal audit, and monitors and makes recommendations to shareholders to appoint and remove external auditors.

4.11 The Board is responsible for the company's system of internal control and for reviewing its effectiveness. It produces an annual statement which is required to state that there is an ongoing process for identifying, evaluating and managing the significant risks faced by the company and that the process has been regularly reviewed and conforms to the Turnbull Guidance.

Theory Revision Questions

The questions in this section are intended to assist you with learning the relevant concepts relating to corporate governance. It is important to memorise and learn these concepts and tools for later recall in the examination. After studying this section, you should attempt the questions in Sections 2 and 3. Questions in Sections 2 and 3 enable you to apply these concepts and tools in composite business problem scenarios. The examination is designed around composite scenario problem solving type questions and Sections 2 and 3 have informed mainly on past exam papers as examples for you to prepare appropriately.

4.1 List and describe the two models of corporate governance.

4.2 List and briefly describe the chronological development of corporate governance in the UK leading to the *Combined Code* currently in use.

4.3 Discuss the key objectives and implications of the Sarbanes-Oxley Act introduced in the USA in 2002.

4.4 Define corporate governance.

4.5 Elaborate on the approach known as "comply or explain".

4.6 What are the main principles of corporate governance in the Combined Code?

4.7 What are the main principles in the Combined Code that relate to Directors?

4.8 Compare and contrast the roles of management and the Audit Committee in relation to internal control.

4.9 What is the Audit Committee's role in relation to internal audit?

4.10 What are the major components of Board effectiveness?

4.11 What information about a company's corporate governance arrangements should be disclosed in the company's annual report to shareholders?

4.12 Define Board effectiveness in terms of the *Combined Code*.

4.13 Contrast the roles of chairman and chief executive in terms of the *Combined Code*.

4.14 List and describe Higgs's suggestions for good practice in respect of non-executive directors.

4.15 List the factors that, render independence of a director unlikely.

4.16 What is the role of the remuneration committee?

4.17 What is the role of the nomination committee?

4.18 What is the primary function of the Audit Committee?

4.19 What are the main roles and responsibilities of the audit committee?

4.20 What are the benefits of good corporate governance?

☑ Theory Revision Solutions

4.1 The corporate governance models are:

1 Shareholder value/agency
2 Stakeholder value

Shareholder value-based corporate governance models single out the shareholder as the affected party and dictates controls and disclosure directed at protecting the shareholders' interests.

Stakeholder value-based corporate governance models recognise interests held by others in addition to the shareholder community and integrates social, environmental and economic aspects of organisational activities for control and disclosure.

4.2 1992 – The Cadbury Report on Financial Aspects of Corporate Governance followed corporate failures including Polly Peck, BCCI, Maxwell Group.

1995 – Greenbury report on Director's Remuneration.

1998 – Hempel report in pursuit of the implementation of the Cadbury report leading to the Corporate Governance *Combined Code*.

1999 – The Institute of Chartered Accountants in England & Wales issued the Turnbull Guidance which was substantially integrated into the *Combined Code*.

2003 – The Higgs report on the role of non-executive directors and, Smith report on the role of audit committees were both issued and integrated into the *Combined Code*.

4.3 The core objectives of the Sarbanes-Oxley (SOX) Act are to promote transparency, integrity and oversight of financial markets. The CEO and CFO are required to certify annual and quarterly financial reports and give assurances regarding effectiveness of internal controls with criminal penalties the consequence of false certifications. The focus of SOX is with financial reporting rather than with risk management and internal control more generally.

4.4 Corporate governance is the System by which companies are directed and controlled. Boards of directors are responsible for the governance of their companies. The shareholders' role in governance is to appoint the directors and the auditors and to satisfy themselves that an appropriate governance structure is in place. The responsibilities of the board include setting the company's strategic aims, providing the leadership to put them into effect, supervising the management of the business and reporting to shareholders on their stewardship. The board's actions are subject to laws, regulations and their shareholders in general meeting (CIMA *Official Terminology*).

4.5 The "comply or explain" approach adopted by the UK Stock Exchange Listing Rules requires of listed companies to comply with the Combined Code on Corporate Governance or explain in their financial statements all deviations and the reasons for such deviation.

4.6 The main principles of corporate governance in the Combined Code relate to:

- Directors
- Remuneration of directors
- Accountability and audit

- Relations with shareholders
- Institutional shareholders
- Disclosure of corporate governance arrangements in annual reports.

4.7   The principles of the Code relating to Directors are:

- The success of the company is dependent on having an effective Board.
- There should be a clear division of responsibilities between the executive who runs the company's business and the Chairman who runs the Board.
- The Board should have a balance of executive and non-executive directors.
- There should be a formal and transparent process for appointing new Directors, who should receive induction and ongoing training.
- The Board should receive information in a timely manner to enable it to discharge its responsibilities effectively.
- Directors should have their own performance evaluated annually, as well as the performance of committees.
- Directors should be re-elected at regular intervals subject to satisfactory performance and succession planning should enable new Directors to refresh the Board.

4.8   Management is responsible for identifying, assessing, managing and monitoring risk and for developing, operating and monitoring the system of internal control. The Audit Committee should receive reports from management on the effectiveness of the internal control systems and the results of testing by internal and external auditors.

4.9   The Audit Committee should review and approve the work of the internal audit function. In doing so, it should appoint the Head of Internal Audit (who should be accountable to the Audit Committee), ensure internal audit has access to the information and resources it needs, approve the scope of work of internal audit, receive regular reports of the results of audits, review management's responses to internal audit recommendations, and monitor the effectiveness of the internal audit function. The Audit Committee should also meet with the internal auditor at least once a year without management being present, to discuss any issues arising from the audit.

4.10   The major contributing factors to an effective Board are:

- Separating the roles of Chairman and Chief Executive.
- Effective non-executive Directors.
- Effective audit, remuneration and nomination committees.

4.11   Schedule C of the Code relating to disclosure states that the following should be included in the annual report:

- A statement of how the board operates, including a high level statement of the types of decisions that are taken by the board and those that are delegated to management.
- The names of the chairman, deputy chairman, chief executive, senior independent director and chairmen and members of the nomination, audit and review and remuneration committees.
- The number of meetings of the board and the committees listed above and individual attendance by directors.

- The names of the non-executive directors who the board determines to be independent, with reasons where necessary.
- Other significant commitments of the chairman.
- Hall performance evaluation of the board, its committees and its directors has been conducted.
- The steps the board has taken to ensure that directors develop an understanding of the views of major shareholders about the company.
- A description of the work of the nomination, remuneration and audit committees.

4.12 The supporting principle for Code A1 states:

The board's role is to provide entrepreneurial leadership of the company within the framework of prudent and effective controls which enables risk to be assessed and managed. The board should set the company's strategic aims, ensure that the necessary financial and human resources are in place for the company to meet its objectives and review management performance. The board should set the company's values and standards and ensure that its obligations to its shareholders and others are understood and met.

4.13 The chairman is responsible for the leadership and effectiveness of the board and effective communication with shareholders. The chairman should be independent. The CEO is responsible for the running of the company's business. Only in exceptional circumstances should a CEO become chairman. The role of chairman and CEO should not vest within one individual.

4.14 Higgs' suggestions for good practice identified the role of non-executive directors in relation to:

- *Strategy*: Non-executive directors are expected to constructively challenge and help to develop proposals on strategy.
- *Performance*: Non-executive directors are required to scrutinise management's performance in meeting agreed goals and monitor performance reporting.
- *Risk*: Non-executive directors should satisfy themselves about the integrity of financial information and that financial controls and systems of risk management are robust and defensible.
- *People*: Non-executive directors are required to determine appropriate levels of remuneration of executive directors, and fulfil the primary role of appointing and removing executive directors, and in succession planning.

4.15 In terms of Code provision A3 independence is unlikely if the director:

- Has been an employee of the company within the last five years;
- Has had a material business relationship with the company within the last three years;
- Has received additional remuneration, participates in share options, performance-related pay or is a member of the company's pension scheme;
- Has close family ties with the company's advisers, directors or senior employees;
- Holds cross-directorships with other directors;
- Represents a significant shareholder;
- Has served on the board for more than nine years.

4.16 The role of the remuneration committee is to determine and agreed with the board the framework for the remuneration of the chief executive, the chairman and other members of the executive management that the board considers should be considered by this committee.

4.17 The role of the nomination committee is to identify and nominate candidates to fill board vacancies when they arise, by evaluating the balance of skills, knowledge and experience on the board and preparing a description of the role and capabilities required for an appointment. (Higgs Suggestions for Good Practice)

4.18 The primary function of the audit committee is to assist the board to fulfil its stewardship responsibilities by reviewing the systems of internal control, the external audit process, the work of the internal audit and the financial information which is provided to shareholders.

4.19 The terms of reference for the audit committee should include at least the following:

- Monitoring the integrity of the company's financial statements, significant judgements made in relation to the financial statements and formal announcements made by the company to the stock exchange.
- Reviewing the company's internal control and risk management systems (although in some cases financial controls may be the responsibility of the audit committee while non-financial controls and risk management may be the responsibility of a separate risk committee of the board, in which case the principals in Code provision C3.1 should also apply to the risk committee).
- Monitoring and reviewing the effectiveness of the internal audit function.
- Making recommendations to the board for the board to place a resolution before shareholders in an annual general meeting for the appointment, re-appointment and removal of the external auditor and to approve the terms of engagement and remuneration of the external auditor.
- Reviewing and monitoring the external auditor's independence and objectivity and the effectiveness of the audit process.
- Developing and implementing policy on the engagement of the external auditors supply non-audit services in order to maintain auditor objectivity and independence.

4.20 The benefits of good corporate governance are:

- Reduced risk
- Stimulated performance
- Improved access to capital markets
- Enhanced marketability of products/services by creating confidence amongst stakeholders
- Improved leadership
- Improved evidence of transparency and accountability.

Risk and Risk Management

Risk and Risk Management

5

LEARNING OUTCOMES

After completing this chapter in the CIMA *Learning System* you should be able to

- define and identify risks facing an organisation;
- explain ways of measuring and assessing risks facing an organisation, including the organisation's ability to bear such risks;
- discuss the purposes and importance of risk management for an organisation;
- evaluate risk management strategies.

Theory Highlights from CIMA Official Study System

5.1 The core of the syllabus for Management Accounting Risk and Control Strategy is dealt with in this chapter. As a consequence this chapter is critical and the theory will be utilised in all other chapters of this course.

5.2 Risk can be defined as 'a chance or possibility of danger, loss, injury or other adverse consequences'. (Typical dictionary definition).

The CIMA *Official terminology* defines risk as: *A condition in which there exists a quantifiable despersion in the possible outcomes from any activity*. By contrast, CIMA *Official terminology* defines uncertainty as: *The inability to predict the outcome from an activity due to a lack of information about the required input/output relationships or about the environment within which the activity takes place.*

5.3 The meaning of risk in the Risk and Control Strategy syllabus, which is consistent with the Turnbull Code (part of the Combined Code on Corporate Governance) is not limited to negative events but explicitly includes the risk of not achieving organisational objectives.

5.4 Risk can be classified in various ways. In order to manage and control risk, we need to endeavour to fully understand its component parts and develop tools to measure each of them. The *Learning System* describes various classification methods although there is no universal classification system for risk. Identifying risk categories depends on the nature of the industry and business circumstances. The advantages of risk classification are that common risks can be managed by similar controls; it forces managers to be more pro-active and enables a 'big picture' of risks; helps managers to apply their experience in finding tools to manage risk; and provides a framework of responsibility for managing risks. A risk management system would be difficult to develop without classifying risks into groups.

5.5 One such classification method is Risk classified by TYPE:

5.5.1 *Business or operational risk* which relates to the activities carried out within an organisation.

5.5.2 *Financial risk* which relates to funding and investment activities.

5.5.3 *Environmental risk* which relates to political, economic, social and the financial environment.

5.5.4 *Reputational risk* which relates to the failure to address other risks.

5.6 We can look at risk in many ways including:

5.6.1 Looking at risk then from both a threat and opportunity perspective, management can determine the drivers of both value and risk and devise measurementand treatment accordingly. Accepting that risk is fundamental to the process of operations, management teams that investigate opportunities potentially resulting from risk situations are better empowered to develop strategic positioning advantage.

5.6.2 The impact of societal, national and organisational culture all have a determining impact upon the profile, severity and treatment of the various types of -risks. Organisations operating globally are substantially affected by these cultural implications and, therefore, the study of culture, its impact and our ability to determine measurements and treatments become more pronounced.

5.6.3 The four rationalities of Adams depicted in Figure 5.2 of the *Learning System* show how different types of people perceive risks quite differently.

5.6.4 This leads us to focus on managers themselves and their culturally determined orientation towards risk. Adams explains the individual's propensity to take risks and discusses the role of potential rewards in their decision-making and behaviour. 'Accident' losses are the consequence of risk taking. Figure-5.3 in the Learning System depicts the process of Adam's risk thermostat with cultural filters. While this model facilitates understanding of the cultural influences, we require more quantifiable measurements to enable evaluation and selection.

5.7 There are numerous definitions for risk management. Relevant definitions for this course include:

5.7.1 According to the CIMA *Official Terminology*, risk management is defined as: The process of understanding and managing the risks that the organization is inevitably subject to in attempting to achieve its corporate objectives (CIMA *Official Terminology*).

5.7.2 The Institute of Risk Management defines risk management as: "The process by which organizations methodically address the risks attached to their activities with the goal of achieving sustained benefit within each activity and across the portfolio of these-activities. The focus of good risk management is the identification and treatment of these risks. Its objective is to add maximum sustainable value to all the activities of the organization.

It marshals the understanding of the potential upside and downside of all those factors which can affect the organization. It increases the probability of success, and reduces both the probability of failure and the uncertainty of achieving the organization's overall objectives."

5.7.3 COSO defines risk management as: "A process, effected by an entity's board of directors, management and other personnel, applied in strategy setting and across the enterprise, designed to identify potential events that may affect the entity, and manage risks to be within its risk appetite, to provide reasonable assurance regarding the achievement of entity's objectives."

5.7.4 Enterprise risk management aligns risk management with strategy and embeds a risk management culture into business operations, seeing risks as opportunities to be grasped for which there are rewards, as well as hazards to be avoided.

5.8 The benefits of risk management are:

- being seen as profitable and successful
- being seen as predictable, with stock market analysts comfortable with what the organization is saying
- not issuing profit warnings or reporting major exceptional adjustments
- goodwill that is not impaired
- mergers and acquisitions that are integrated effectively
- excellent brand reputation
- being seen as socially responsible
- having a well-managed supply chain
- having a good credit rating.

5.9 There are several different models for risk management. The Institute of Risk Management's standard depicted in Figure 5.7 of the *Learning System* identifies the following steps:

5.9.1 Carry out risk assessment through identification, description and estimation. Many methods exist for identifying risk including workshops, brainstorming, benchmarking, scenario analysis, etc. Risk description involves defining the nature of risk, risk treatment possibilities, etc (see Table 5.1 in the *Learning System* for an example). Risk can be estimated using surveys, scenarios, simulations, probabilities, Delphi, etc. Whilst many of these methods aim to be scientific and try to develop quantifiable measures, risk assessment is often a subjective exercise based on experience, intuition and judgement.

5.9.2 The risk register is the most common method of recording risks and the likelihood/consequences matrix is one of the most common methods of estimating risk.

5.9.3 Risk reporting takes place before and after risk treatment and shows the gross risk (before treatment) and net or residual risk (after treatment).

5.9.4 Risk treatment (or risk response) may involve avoidance, reduction, sharing or acceptance.

Theory Revision Questions

The questions in this section are intended to assist you with learning the relevant concepts relating to risk and risk management. It is important to memorise and learn these concepts and tools for later recall in the examination. After studying this section, you should attempt the questions in Sections 2 and 3. Questions in Sections 2 and 3 enable you to apply these concepts and tools in composite business problem scenarios. The examination is designed around composite scenario problem solving type questions and Sections 2 and 3 have informed mainly on past exam papers as examples for you to prepare appropriately.

5.1 List ways in which risk can be classified and briefly describe each one.

5.2 List examples of operational risk.

5.3 List examples of financial risk.

5.4 List examples of environmental risk.

5.5 Explain Reputational risk using an example.

5.6 List examples of economic risk.

5.7 List examples of political risk.

5.8 Define risk in the sense that it is used in the Risk and Control syllabus.

5.9 List examples of risk as a hazard.

5.10 List examples of risk as a threat.

5.11 List examples of risk as opportunity.

5.12 The Institute of Risk Management categorises risk in terms of financial, strategic, operational and hazard. For each of these categories, list the externally driven risks.

5.13 The Institute of Risk Management categorises risk in terms of financial, strategic, operational and hazard. For each of these categories, list the internally driven risks.

5.14 Discuss the role of Culture in risk taking by managers.

5.15 Weber and Hsee proposed a "cushion hypothesis" following a study involving American, German, Polish and Chinese nationals. Explain the effect of this cushion on organisational decision-maker behaviour.

5.16 Discuss the four rationalities together with possible implications for seeing risk as proposed by Adams (1995).

5.17 Described "risk appetite" in an organisational context.

5.18 Explain the difference between explicit and implicit knowledge.

5.19 What is the CIMA definition of risk management?

5.20 Discuss enterprise risk management in terms of the COSO definition.

5.21 The shareholders of an organisation are the ultimate risk bearers. Discuss risk management in terms of shareholder value.

5.22 Discuss the four stages of shareholder value creation as defined by Ernst & Young (2001).

5.23 List the benefits of risk management.

5.24 List benefits specific to enterprise risk management.

5.25 Distinguish between highly integrated and highly dispersed risk management architecture and list eight benefits of the highly integrated option.

5.26 List the elements of a risk management framework.

5.27 In order for risk management to be effective, resourcing has to ensure coverage of a number of functions. List these functions.

5.28 With a specific focus on ensuring the effective functioning of risk management, list the requirements to be considered in the resourcing decision-making process.

5.29 Discuss key human behaviour control measures that are necessary to reinforce an appropriate risk management culture.

5.30 Draw the diagram of the CIMA risk management cycle.

5.31 List methods of identifying risk.

5.32 List methods that can be deployed to measure risk.

5.33 Discuss the key limitations of risk measurement.

5.34 Discuss the likelihood/consequences matrix in relation to risk evaluation.

5.35 What should risk reporting be comprised of and what should it address?

5.36 List the four different responses to risk.

☑ Theory Revision Solutions

5.1 Four ways in which risk can be classified are:

1 *Business or operational risk* relates to the activities carried out within an organisation.
2 *Financial risk* relates to the financial/investment/funding operations of an organisation.
3 *Environmental risk* relates to changes in the political, economic, social and operating environment.
4 *Reputational risk* relates to the impact upon the image/name/reputation of the organisation and is caused by a failure to adequately address other risks.

5.2 Examples of operational risk include:

Business interruption
Errors of commission or omission by employees
Product failure
Health and safety
Failure of IT or mechanised systems
Fraud
Loss of key people
Litigation
Loss of suppliers.

5.3 Examples of financial risk include:

- *Credit risk*: The risk of not being paid by customers.
- *Liquidity risk*: The risk of running out of money.
- *Currency risk*: The risk of change in the exchange rate when trading internationally.
- *Interest rate risk*: The risk of interest rate change.

5.4 Examples of environmental risk include:

Legislative change
Regulations (Industry and government in many instances)
Climate change
Natural disasters
Loss of business
Competition
Economic slowdown
Stock market fluctuations.

5.5 Numerous instances worldwide of banks experiencing a run on withdrawals is a result of a loss of confidence by the clients of that bank followed by their withdrawal of funds in order to limit their own risk of potential loss.

In many instances like this, the end result of a run on the bank leads to complete failure of the bank.

5.6 Examples of economic risk, in terms of international operations, include:

- Loss of business for not dealing with suppliers and customers in the host country currency.
- Loss of income due to exchange rate movements where fixed price contracts are quoted in the currency of the host country.

- Lower than planned return on investment from a foreign direct investment project because of unexpected economic slowdown in that country.
- Investing in the home country, a decision which is subsequently affected by changes in relative exchange rates between the home country and markets in other countries.

5.7 Examples of political risks include:

- Loss of land, plant and equipment due to nationalisation of foreign-owned business interests in a host country after regime change.
- Change in regulation in a foreign country requiring specific use of local materials or labour.
- Cash flow implications as a result of the imposition of exchange controls by a foreign country in which the company trades.
- Loss of profits due to changes in tax rate in a foreign country in which the company trades.

5.8 Risk as it is used in the Risk and Control syllabus can be understood as hazard or threat, i.e. negative or downside events. Risk can also be seen as uncertainty, reflected in the CIMA *Official Terminology* definition where there are many possible outcomes, both positive and negative. Risk as opportunity is based on the risk/return tradeoff and using techniques to maximise the positive and minimise the negative. Each view of risk is the responsibility of different managers, but all comprise risk as it is used in the syllabus.

5.9 Risk as hazard includes:

- The risk of fire
- The risk of failure of an IT system
- The risk of loss of life or injury on a construction site
- The risk of loss of plots and equipment due to flooding.

NOTE: The examples of risk, in their various classifications in questions 9 to 11, are not exhaustive. There are many more examples of each.

5.10 Risk as a threat includes:

- Possible entry into a market by a competitor
- Possible loss of customers or market due to a competitor introducing a new technology
- Potential loss of supply of inputs as a result of contractual changes with a supplier
- Potential loss of business due to changes in bilateral agreements between countries in which the organisation trades.

5.11 Risk as an opportunity includes:

- Taking over a competitor that is struggling. The opportunity here is to deploy the company's skills and resources to overcome the weaknesses in the competitors business to increase the earnings of the combined organisation.
- Entering a new market.

Taking a product into a new market could result in failure. It is therefore risky and, where such risk is managed with skill, it could result in a positive outcome and gain for the company. In entering this new market, however, to extract opportunity, the management and measurement of possible negative outcomes is imperative.

- Investing in a new manufacturing facility.
- Launching a new technology.

 The launch of WAP technology was not very successful in the marketplace even though it was groundbreaking at the time. While the returns from WAP itself were small or even negative, it led to the discovery of related market needs and the introduction of MMS etc.

5.12 The externally driven hazards, according to the Institute of Risk Management, are as follows:

- Financial risks:
  - Interest rates
  - Foreign exchange
  - Credit
- Strategic risks:
  - Competition
  - Customer changes
  - Industry changes
  - Customer demand
- Operational risks:
  - Regulations
  - Culture
  - Board composition
- Hazard risks:
  - Contracts
  - Natural events
  - Suppliers
  - Environment

5.13 The internally driven hazards, according to the Institute of Risk Management, are as follows:

- Financial risks:
  - Liquidity and cash flow
- Strategic risks:
  - M & A integration
  - Research and development
  - Intellectual capital
- Operational risks:
  - Accounting controls
  - Information systems
  - Recruitment
  - Supply chain
- Hazard risks:
  - Public access
  - Employees
  - Properties
  - Products and services.

5.14 "Bettis and Thomas (1990) have shown that researchers have very little knowledge about how managers in organizations perceive and take risks." This statement, taken from the Learning System by Collier and Mgyei-Ampomah (2005), demonstrates the extent to which, in the 21st century, we still have some way to go in understanding risk, risk taking and risk appetite in the decision-making process.

From the work done by Douglas and Wildavsky (1983) it is clear that culture plays a significant role. They found that: "... each culture, each set of shared values in supporting social institutions is biased toward highlighting certain risks and downplaying others.

Weber & Milliman (1997) found that risk taking could be a stable personality trait but that situational variables may be the results of changes in risk perception.

March and Shapira (1987) identified three motivations for risk-taking:

1   Managers saw risk-taking as essential to success in decision-making;
2   Managers associated risk-taking with the expectations of their jobs rather than with any personal preference for risk;
3   Managers recognised the 'emotional pleasures and pain' of risk taking.

When dealing with the human factor, risk management becomes substantially more difficult due to our inability to measure and, therefore, manage the risk decision-making process. Managing the risk-taking decision-making process enters the realm of uncertainty due to this lack of ability to measure or predict likely outcomes and the intuitive (or gut-feel) subjective approach to control becomes the norm.

5.15   The effect of the "cushion hypothesis" proposed by Weber and Hsee (1998) is to cushion members [of the organisation] against the consequences of negatives outcomes. As a result of this cushion effect, decision-makers perception of the riskiness of options is distorted.

5.16   Adams (1995) describes four rationalities that have implications for how people perceive risk. These rationalities, together with possible implications, are detailed as follows:

- *Fatalists*: Have minimal control over their own lives and, therefore, the management of risk is irrelevant to them. The implications of risk will have little meaning for these individuals.
- *Hierarchists*: Organize their world with strong group boundaries and structured relationships in hierarchial fashion. They adopt a bureaucratic risk management style using various risk management techniques. People with this orientation are likely to receive risk as managed through compliance with rules and regulations. The perception of risk will be distorted to a greater or lesser extent depending upon whether or not it is perceived to be addressed by compliance methods contained in the "handbook".
- *Individualists*: Are free thinking individuals who strive to exert control over their environment. Typically, they are self-made people and are an small–medium enterprise entrepreneurs. These individuals are more likely to weigh and understand the possible outcomes of risk. They are, however, less risk averse than people subscribing to other rationalities.
- *Egalitarians*: Have strong group loyalties. They arrived at decisions democratically and have little respect for externally imposed rules. The implications for risk taking and decision-making could be that they respond to slowly and/or disregard the risk implications. They will be most comfortable in a risk-sharing situation (e.g. insurance, hedging or transfer to other organisations).

5.17 Risk appetite describes the amount of risk an organisation is willing to accept in pursuit of value. It is directly related to an organisation's strategy. Risk appetite could be expressed as the acceptable balance between growth, risk and return.

5.18 Explicit knowledge is knowledge which can be recorded and shared while implicit knowledge can be learned and executed by an individual that cannot be recorded or directly shared. (e.g. Learning how to ride a bicycle has to be done directly by each individual and is therefore an implicit knowledge while, once designed, the building of a rocket can be recorded and shared.)

5.19 CIMA define risk management as:

The process of understanding and managing the risks that the organisation is inevitably subject to in attempting to achieve its corporate objectives. (CIMA *Official Terminology*)

5.20 COSO define enterprise risk management as:

A process, effected by an entity's board of directors, management and other personnel, applied in strategy setting and across the enterprise, designed to identify potential events that may affect the entity, and manage risks to be within its risk appetite, to provide reasonable assurance regarding the achievement of entity's objectives.

Enterprise risk management is that group of risks that are derived from decisions taken by the management and personnel of an organisation in setting strategy, structuring and resourcing the organisation and operating the system. Enterprise risk should thus be seen as the appetite to undertake risks by an organisation (wittingly or unwittingly) that enable the exploitation of opportunities and, simultaneously, expose the stakeholders to risks associated with those actions.

5.21 Ernst & Young (2001) model shareholder value as being: *the static NPV of existing business model + Value of future growth options.*

The above is more simply described in the Learning System as: "it's the sum of the value of what the company does now and the value of what they could possibly do in the future".

From these definitions we can deduct that shareholders take risks with the view to unlocking value. The risk profile of an organisation for shareholders therefore comprises the perceived present value of the business as it is configured at present plus the value (both positive and negative) of future growth/decline that is undertaken by the directors and management of the organisation.

5.22 Ernst & Young have identified four stages in the process of good risk management to enable business to exploit opportunities for future growth while protecting the value already created. These four stages are as follows:

1 Established what shareholders value about the company – through talking with the investment community and linking value creation processes to key performance indicators.
2 Identify the risks around the key shareholder value drivers – the investment community can identify those factors that will influence the valuation of the company. All other risks will also be considered, even if not known by investors.
3 Determine the preferred treatment for the risks – the investment community can give their views on what actions they would like management to take in relation

to the risks. The risk/reward trade-off can be quantified by estimating the change in the company's market valuation if a particular risk treatment was implemented.

4 Communicate risk treatments to shareholders – shareholders need to be well informed, as a shareholder vision is important in relation to the inter-related concepts of risk management and shareholder value.

5.23 The benefits of risk management include:

- Being seen as profitable and successful
- Being seen as predictable (e.g. comply with corporate governance requirements)
- Having fewer exceptional items and profit warnings
- Empowered to manage events proactively (e.g. mergers and acquisitions)
- Intangible assets are less likely to be impaired (e.g. trade names, goodwill and brand reputation)
- Works in favour of good-corporate-citizenship reputation
- Improved supply chain management
- Better credit ratings all possible.

5.24 The benefits of enterprise risk management include:

- Aligning risk appetite with strategic plan
- Balancing growth, risk and return
- Improving response to risk decisions
- Reducing operational surprises and losses
- Improved control of enterprise-wide/cross-enterprise risks
- Improved risk management through decisions and responses based upon integrated multiple risk information
- Improved access to identify and seize opportunities
- Opportunity to improve capital rationing decisions in favour of efficient risk attenuation and opportunity exploitation.

5.25 A highly integrated approach to risk architecture in an organisation would see all business units:

- Sharing a common language
- Sharing tools and techniques
- Executing shared periodic assessment of total risk.

The highly integrated approach to risk is particularly effective when risk factors are common across functional and business units.

By contrast, the highly dispersed approach to risk architecture is more appropriate to organisations where business units differ substantially in terms of their risk profiles and where operations differ substantially.

The integrated approach is generally regarded as best practice and, according to IFAC, includes the following:

1 Organization-wide acceptance of the risk management framework
2 Commitment from executives and the board of directors
3 Has an established risk response strategy
4 Has assigned responsibility for risk management change processes
5 Is adequately resourced
6 Comprises comprehensive communication structures
7 Risk cultures are reinforced through human resource mechanisms
8 The risk management process is monitored.

5.26 The risk management framework can be described as comprising the following elements:

> Risk management policy
> Resourcing risk management
> Implementation of risk management
> Risk management review and reporting.

5.27 In order for risk management to be effective, it should be driven by the board. The board, in turn, should ensure that an appropriate group of executives manage the process. The functions that require management are:

- Primary advocacy for risk management
- Policy, framework and methodology is necessary for each business unit to identify, analyse and manage their risks more effectively
- Development and execution of response processes to risk threat or event
- Assessment and auditing of the adequacy of risk responses
- The facilitation, challenge and leading of risk management
- Control of the risk management process ensuring that policy and strategy are operating effectively
- Trouble-shooting and corrective action functions
- Feedback and reporting requirements within the executive and to the board.

A key point to note here is that there is a clear message to management: risk management requires specific resourcing that is not subordinated (or appended) to operational line processes. Specific attention should be paid to ensure that effective risk management is implemented and resourced.

5.28 Management should specifically ensure that they deal with the following with regards to establishing an effective risk management system:

- The cost of providing the resources including additional support required to ensure its correct implementation has to be determined.
- Skills and experience are required to ensure that all aspects of risk exposure are covered adequately.
- Since human resources are the primary source of competitive advantage and, simultaneously a substantial contributor to business risks, career and succession planning is key.
- Provide adequate infrastructure and human resources to ensure constructive relationships are built between business units.
- Knowledge is assembled and managed.

Without these resources, risk management cannot be effective, leaving the organisation venerable to risk events.

5.29 In order for people to behave appropriately to ensure the containment and management of risk, careful attention has to be paid to the following key areas:
- Corporate culture influenced, over time, to ensure adoption of formal rules-based and informal values-based practices
- Appropriate job design
  Performance measurement
  Delegation enforcement of accountabilities
  Appropriate incentives and rewards.

5.30

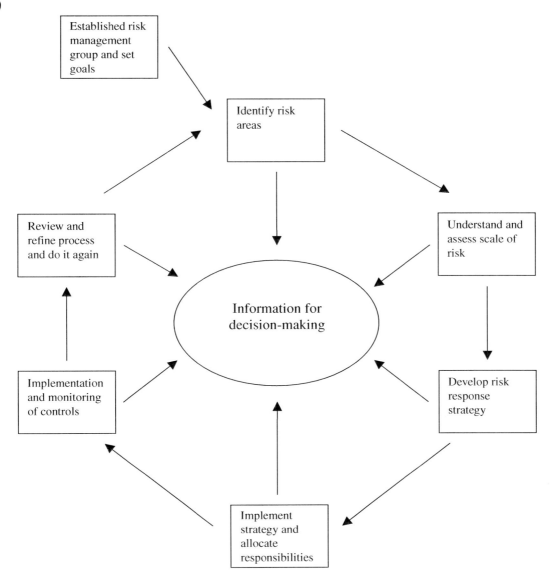

CIMA risk management cycle
Source: Chartered Institute of Management Accountants (2002), *Risk Management: A guide to Good Practice*, CIMA

5.31 Twelve methods of identifying risk include:

1 Brainstorming
2 Workshops
3 Stakeholder consultations
4 Benchmarking
5 Checklists
6 Scenario analysis
7 Incident investigation
8 Auditing and inspection
9 Hazard and operability studies
10 Fishbone analysis
11 Questionnaires/surveys
12 Interviews.

5.32 Risk can be estimated by deploying one or more of the following methods:

1 Information gathering
2 Scenario planning
3 Soft systems analysis
4 Computer simulations (Monte Carlo technique)
5 Decision trees
6 Root cause analysis
7 Fault tree/event tree analysis
8 Dependency modeling
9 Failure mode and effect analysis
10 Human reliability analysis
11 Sensitivity analysis
12 Cost-benefit and risk-benefit analysis
13 Real options modeling
14 Delphi method
15 Risk mapping
16 SWOT
17 PEST
18 HAZOP
19 Statistical inference (Regression analysis)
20 Measures of central tendency and dispersion.

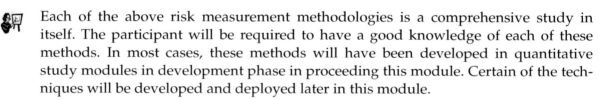 Each of the above risk measurement methodologies is a comprehensive study in itself. The participant will be required to have a good knowledge of each of these methods. In most cases, these methods will have been developed in quantitative study modules in development phase in proceeding this module. Certain of the techniques will be developed and deployed later in this module.

5.33 The key limitations of known risk measurements include:

- *Reductionist*: Many of the methods, although formal and structured, rely on assumptions and specific focus or selection for their measurement to be reliable. If the given assumptions are violated, the measure could be inaccurate. They rely on linear cause-and-effect relationships which are not necessarily a true reflection of the prevailing risk condition.
- *Subjectivity*: A number of the methods rely upon individual perceptions which, in themselves, are unreliable when an attempt is made to apply them to generalisation.
- *Combined reductionist and subjectivity*: These methods suffer the effects of both of the abovementioned limitations.

What we observe here is that there exists an inherent risk in the risk measurement methodology itself, let alone the original risk condition we are attempting to measure. The participant is alerted to be aware of the severity of these shortcomings and to deploy multiple measurement methods wherever possible and to systemise the risk management process in order to build upon past experiences and outcomes so as to develop a comprehensive database to enhance the organisational knowledge surrounding risk and its management.

5.34 The likelihood/consequence matrix approach to risk evaluation can have varying degrees of ranking dependent upon the approach taken by the organisation. The primary focus of this matrix is to categorise risks according to severity on the one hand

and likelihood on the other in order to separate risk conditions along the lines of significance. This has the effect of reducing the number of risk conditions to be considered at each organisational level and promotes the focusing of attention on those risk areas that are the most likely to result in severe loss.

5.35   Risk reporting should include:

- A systematic review of the risk forecast carried out at least annually;
- A review of the management responses to the significant risks and risk strategy;
- A monitoring and feedback loop on action taken and variance in the assessment of the significant risks;
- An early warning system to indicate material change in the risk profile, or circumstances, which could increase exposure or threaten areas of opportunity;
- The inclusion of audit work as part of the communication and reporting process.

Risk reporting should address the following:

- The control systems that have been put in place for risk management;
- The process is used to identify and respond to risks;
- The methods used to manage significant risks;
- A description of the monitoring and review system.

5.36   Risk treatment (or risk response) is the process of selecting and implementing measures to modify risk. Risk responses may include:

- Avoidance
- Reduction
- Sharing
- Acceptance.

Internal Control

Internal Control

6

LEARNING OUTCOMES

After completing this chapter you should be able to

- discuss the purposes and importance of internal control for an organisation;
- evaluate risk management strategies;
- evaluate the essential features of internal control systems for identifying, assessing and managing risks;
- evaluate the costs and benefits of a particular internal control system.

Theory Highlights from CIMA Official Study System

6.1 Organisations face the external and internal environments of two dimensions namely: controllable and uncontrollable conditions. This chapter discusses the role of internal controls within the organisation that are prescribed on the one hand by legislation and executed by the executive on the other for the purposes of containing risk and managing strategic objectives.

6.2 There are various definitions of internal control systems. In general, the systems approach is applied to internal controls even though various institutions place a greater or lesser emphasis upon quantifiable measurements. In general, internal control is action oriented with board and executive responsibility for achieving the organisation's strategic objectives.

6.3 The US COSO and UK Combined Code are examples of state/industry measures to promote the implementation and maintenance of internal control measures within organisations. These governance documents prescribe processes and disclosure/reporting requirements that compel the organisation to implement and effect control measures.

6.4 Internal controls can be classified as being financial and non-financial quantitative measures on the one hand and qualitative measures on the other. Much more attention is being paid lately to the qualitative aspects of organisations measurement and monitoring environment. Academics, practitioners and executives increasingly place more emphasis upon qualitative and non-financial measures in addition to well-developed financial measures in order to measure and manage organisational activities, resources and environment in order to achieve the objectives of the designed strategy.

6.5 Risks, together with costs, client and supplier relationships, resource management and knowledge of the domain of the board, executive management and general staff. This shift in emphasis on measurement and control is changing the role of management accountants within the organisation. In the past, accounting departments were seen to be responsible for the recording and interpretation of accounting information. Management accounting is now seen as being: *the application of the principles of accounting and financial management to create, protect, preserve and increase value so as to deliver that value to the stakeholders* (CIMA *Official Terminology*). The management accountants role is evolving into a value adding professional activity directed at supporting and empowering stakeholders within the organisation to make informed decisions, based upon sound accounting information, in order to develop, implement and control internal processes in order to achieve strategic objectives.

6.6 This changed role for the management accountant brings about a responsibility to provide up-to-date accounting information and simultaneously factor in non-financial and qualitative aspects and to report these within appropriate time deadlines to internal stakeholders.

6.7 An important characteristic of the new role of management accountants is to monitor the cost-benefit and risk-benefit of collecting data, managing its recording, storage and retrieval process in such a way that value is not destroyed in the process.

6.8 Additional pressures being brought to bear include globalisation, increasing competition, technological change in production and information technology, changing organisational structures, the influences of multi-cultural environments within the workplace and changing perceptions of management with regards to managing change and information needs.

6.9 The management accountant is ideally placed, owing to their professional training that includes analysis of information and systems, to play a significant role in developing and implementing risk management and internal control systems.

6.10 *Internal control is the whole system of controls, financial and otherwise, established to provide reasonable assurance of effective and efficient operation, internal financial control, and compliance with laws and regulation* (CIMA *Official Terminology*).

6.11 An internal control system comprises the control environment (the attitude, awareness and actions of directors and managers regarding the importance of internal controls) and control procedures (the policies and procedures established to achieve the organization's objectives).

6.12 Accounting controls are controls over cash, debtors, inventory, investments, fixed assets, creditors, loans, income and expenses.

⍰ **Theory Revision Questions**

 The questions in this section are intended to assist you with learning the relevant concepts relating to internal control. It is important to memorise and learn these concepts and tools for later recall in the examination. After studying this section, you should attempt the questions in Sections 2 and 3. Questions in Sections 2 and 3 enable you to apply these concepts and tools in composite business problem scenarios. The examination is designed around composite scenario problem solving type questions and Sections 2 and 3 have informed mainly on past exam papers as examples for you to prepare appropriately.

6.1   Define internal control.

6.2   What constitutes an internal control system?

6.3   Discuss the five elements of the COSO model of internal control.

6.4   How does 'The Turnbull Guidance' influence the Combined Code (Financial Reporting Council, 2003)?

6.5   Controls can be classified as falling into three broad categories namely:

- Financial controls
- Non-financial quantitative controls
- Non-financial qualitative controls.

Discuss each of these controls and draw some links with Kaplan & Norton's Balanced Scorecard.

6.6   Discuss the influences that are changing the role of management accountants.

6.7   List the elements of cash control that support risk management.

6.8   Describe the elements of debtors control and its impact on risk management.

6.9   What inventory controls should be implemented to manage risk?

6.10 What role does investment practice play in organisational risk?

6.11 What methods can minimise the risk of losses and damage to fixed assets?

6.12 List appropriate ways to control Creditors risk.

6.13 What controls are recommended for revenue and expense risk management?

6.14 What controls can be applied to limit payroll related losses?

6.15 Describe the limitations of internal controls.

Theory Revision Solutions

6.1 Internal control is the whole system of internal controls, financial and otherwise, established in order to provide reasonable assurance of:

(a) Effective and efficient operation
(b) Internal financial control
(c) Compliance with laws and regulations.
(CIMA *Official Terminology*)

6.2 Definitions of internal control systems, deployed by organisations, are varied. Generally speaking though, they comprise the following key elements:

- Their aim is to provide reasonable assurance that the objectives of the organisation are being met;
- They comprise policies and procedures and safeguards to regulate the behaviour of management and internal stakeholders;
- They are based upon acknowledged management style, corporate culture and values that influence the philosophy, operating style and organisational structure;
- Responsibility vests with the board of directors and management to establish, maintain and control the system.
- They meet the requirements of a system based upon measurable objective setting, control of activity and behaviour and evaluation and assessment leading to a review process.

6.3 The COSO model of internal control (applicable in the USA) comprises five elements as follows:

1 *Control environment* which is defined by CIMA as *"the overall attitude, awareness and actions of directors and management regarding internal controls and their importance to the entity . . . [it] encompasses the management style, and corporate culture and values shared by a war employees. It provides a background against which the various other controls are operated"* (CIMA *Official Terminology*).
2 *Risk assessment* deals with that section of the model directed at identifying the risks of failing to meet financial reporting objectives, failing to meet compliance and failing to meet operational objectives. COSO recommends the identification of external and internal risks to the organisation and its activities.
3 *Control activities* are the policies and procedures that help ensure objectives are achieved and include both accounting and non-accounting controls.
4 *Monitoring* is concerned with the need for management to monitor the entire control system through specific evaluations.
5 *Information and communication* deals with that area of the model concerned with the capture of relevant internal and external information about the competition, economic and regulatory matters and the potential of strategic and integrated information systems.

6.4 While the Combined Code recognises profit as being the reward for successful risk-taking in business, it seeks to regulate how boards and their management effect internal control to manage risk rather than to eliminate it. The Turnbull Guidance extends the requirement to have boards base their approach on sound risk based systems of internal control coupled with the requirement to review its effectiveness.

The Turnbull Guidance extends the requirement under the Combined Code for Boards to centre their approach to internal control on a risk-based platform.

6.5 The Balanced Scorecard extended performance measurement from purely financial measures to include non-financial measures on three perspectives: customer, process and learning and growth (or innovation). These three non-financial measures were seen as leading indicators of financial performance measures which lagged the non-financial measures. Consequently, non-financial measures become used as targets and form part of an internal control system.

 However, financial and non-financial measures are unable to provide a complete set of controls. There are many qualitative (i.e. non quantifiable) controls in business including controls over recruitment, training, induction, day-to-day supervision of work, performance appraisal, rewards and sanctions, policies and procedures, strategic plans, standard operating instructions (and many more).

The whole set of controls within an organisation comprise financial controls, non-financial measures such as contained in a Balanced Scorecard and many different qualitative controls.

6.6 The role of management accountants is *"the application of the principles of accounting and financial management to create, protect, preserve an increase in value so as to deliver that value to the stakeholder"* (CIMA *Official Terminology*). Thus management accounting is more involved with the business and the strategic support perspective (Scapens et al., 2003).

Scapens et al. identified the following changes that have influenced the shift in focus of the management accountant:

- Globalisation, increasing competition, volatile markets and the emergence of more customer-oriented companies;
- Technological change in production and information technology and the nature of work and information flows as a consequence of enterprise resource planning systems and personal computers;
- Changing organisational structures such as demergers and focusing on core competencies and the outsourcing of non-core activities.
- The feeling in top management that change is necessary and the changing management information needs.

These factors have led to a shift in 'ownership' of [management] accounting reports away from accountants to business managers.

 CIMA's Fraud and Risk Management Working Group argues that: *"Management accountants, whose professional training includes the analysis of information and systems, performance and strategic management, can have a significant role to play in developing and implementing risk management and internal control systems within their organizations."* (Chartered Institute of Management Accountants, 2002 p. 3–4).

6.7 Cash control elements that support risk management are:

- Monies received by the organisation are banked;
- Bank accounts exist and a properly safeguarded;
- Bank accounts, especially foreign accounts are properly authorised;

- Signatories for bank accounts are authorised and sufficient
- Payments are properly authorised;
- Transfers between bank accounts are properly accounted for;
- Adequate cash forecasting is carried out to ensure that commitments are recorded and overdraft limits are not exceeded.

6.8   The control over debtors' accounts is crucial to proper risk management.

Debtor controls ensure that:

- Invoicing of customers is properly recorded in debtor accounts;
- Money collected from customers is properly recorded in debtor records;
- Bad debts are written off and adequate provision is made for doubtful debts;
- Debtor accounts are regularly reconciled;
- Appropriate credit checking procedures are in place;
- Collection activity is ongoing and effective;
- Credit notes and write-offs are properly authorised;
- Investigations take place in relation to all disputed amounts with customers;
- Customers verify the balances on their accounts.

6.9   Inventory is a major asset class in many organisations and comprises both potential advantage on the positive side and risk of major loss on the negative side if poorly managed. Control over inventory is essential to ensure that the negative potential is closely managed. Risk management strategies include:

- Periodic physical checks compared with inventory records to ensure that losses are detected and controlled;
- Valuation of inventory is managed in accordance with accounting principles;
- Receipt, dispatch, production and distribution of inventory should be affected the according to robust procedures;
- Security issues with regards to storage and handling all critical if losses and risk of loss are to be contained;
- The suitability of product is determined and obsolete, excess or damaged stock is eliminated according to proper controls and also as a nation;
- Distribution and transit of stock requires stringent procedures including such measures as recipient collaboration audits.

6.10   Treasury activities involving the maintenance of liquidity, investment of idle funds, mergers and acquisitions, interest rate and currency risk strategies all have the potential of enhancing organisational performance or destroying earned profits dependent upon judgement and stringent control measures. Investment on intangibles risks can be contained by deploying the following risk response strategies:

- Audits to verify the physical evidence of ownership of investments and measures to ensure their safe custody;
- Periodic review of all investments to determine their value creation status and to decide upon retention or disposal strategies;
- The establishment and maintenance of acquisition and disposal policies and procedures coupled with appropriate authorisation requirements;
- Amortisation, where appropriate, is applied to ensure correct valuation reporting in accordance with accounting standards.

6.11 With the ever-increasing pace of change, fixed assets designed to unlock future benefits increasingly become liabilities or obsolete. In order to ensure that assets are adequately managed, the following controls should be applied:

- A comprehensive fixed asset register should be maintained and periodically reviewed to ensure that assets are present;
- Acquisitions and disposals are properly authorised;
- Adequate security is provided to prevent theft, damage or misuse;
- Insurance cover exists to compensate for substantial potential losses;
- Assets are adequately depreciated to reflect a reasonable consumption of their value;
- Obsolete and/or worn out assets should be identified and treated appropriately in terms of accounting principles.

6.12 In most organisations, and certainly in trading and manufacturing companies, a large proportion of the company's activities, funds and the resultant acquisition of assets are controlled by staff members dealing with creditors. Control over the risks in this area is maintained through:

- Pre-purchase authorisation policies and procedures followed correctly;
- Purchases properly authorised and issued (in writing);
- Proof-of-delivery procedures implemented and followed to ensure purchased goods are received in good order;
- Procedures are followed to confirm supplier invoice details regarding quantities, price and conditions are checked against the original purchase orders and variances follow policies, procedure and authorisation;
- Invoices are properly recorded in creditors accounts and are reconciled monthly prior to payment requisition processes;
- Payments to suppliers are properly authorised and recorded in creditors accounts;
- Investigations take place, preferably by neutral employees, in situations which arise regarding quality, quantity and pricing issues.

6.13 Revenue, cost of goods sold and expenses constitute the trading and operating activities of an organisation. Controls over these areas to contain risk of loss are required to augment those controls deployed to monitor and control organizational performance. The risk elements can be controlled through:

- Income and expenses are referenced to organisational strategy and objectives through properly maintained budgeting processes.
- Properly documenting sale of goods and services immediately after the transaction occurs.
- Costs are properly recorded and classified.
- Income and expenses are matched and relate to the appropriate accounting period and accruals and prepayments are properly recorded to adjust between periods.
- Authorisation procedures are maintained to ensure that expenses are pre-authorised and that supplier invoices are properly controlled and checked against purchase orders.

6.14 Payroll expenses make up a substantial part of an organisation's expenses and require the following controls to be present to control risk:

- Human resource policies and procedures are established, maintained and followed with regard to recruitment, pre-employment checks and screening processes.

- Proper processes are implemented and followed by departmental managers to ensure that new recruits are properly authorised.
- Rates of pay are in accordance with human resource policies, pay scales and job grades.
- Time worked is properly recorded.
- Annual leave, sick or maternity leave, over time, extras and piecework are properly authorised.
- Employees who terminate employment are removed from the payroll.
- Procedures are established and maintained to verify that employee numbers correlate with the records and that 'ghost' employees are not present.
- Payroll deductions are all properly authorised and accepted by employees and are in compliance with statutory requirements.
- Employee benefits are properly authorised and procedures ensure that payments are regular.

6.15 Internal controls are subject to limitations that should be understood and factored into management behaviour. These limitations include:

1 Management is responsible for the establishment, implementation and maintenance of controls and cannot rely on auditors to review the adequacy of these controls.
2 Robust internal controls can provide a reasonable assurance but are not an absolute guarantee.
3 Independent risk control procedures that are separated from data processing and recordkeeping help enhance reliability. The viability of such an implementation is dependent upon cost–benefit evaluation.
4 There is always the possibility of error or gaps in the accounting system that can be deliberately circumvented or exploited by determined individuals. Management overriding of controls, systems limitations and changed business conditions expose the organisation to risks.

Internal Audit and the Auditing Process

Internal Audit and the Auditing Process

7

LEARNING OUTCOMES

After completing this chapter in the CIMA *Learning System* you should be able to

- explain the importance of management review of controls;
- evaluate the process of internal audit;
- produce a plan for the audit of various organisational activities including, management, accounting and information systems;
- analyse problems associated with the audit of activities and systems, and recommend action to avoid or solve those problems;
- recommend action to improve the efficiency, effectiveness and control of activities;
- discuss the importance of exercising ethical principles in conducting of and reporting on internal reviews.

Theory Highlights from CIMA Official Study System

7.1 This chapter focuses specifically on the internal audit and the auditing process. It is important to position auditing in terms of the role and responsibility borne by the directors and management on the one hand and the auditors on the other. It is also important to distinguish the roles played by internal auditors and external auditors.

7.2 We start by defining audit: A systematic examination of the activities and status of an entity, based primarily on investigation and analysis of its systems, controls and records (CIMA *Official Terminology*).

7.3 Auditing thus constitutes a checking and verification process and not a control process in itself. It is therefore completely inappropriate for management to rely upon internal audit processes to control and manage risk. Instead, management should incorporate audit report outputs into the evaluation and feedback mechanisms used to control and manage risk and rely on those outputs as additional information and feedback regarding the competence and performance of their risk management and control system.

7.4 Audits provide an 'opinion', based on a systematic and rigorous benchmarking process involving observation, interviews, reviews of reports, recalculations and analysis, conducted by a trained specialists. Providing this specialist (auditor) is independent of influences within and from external sources to the organisation, their judgment and commentary can provide an invaluable source of feedback to aid in refining the risk and control processes. The audit process is not a replacement for internal control and risk management.

7.5   Depending on the purpose of the audit, they take various forms and their format, scope and output can vary considerably. The participants should be familiar with the following forms of audit:

    7.5.1   Financial audit
    7.5.2   Compliance audit
    7.5.3   Transactions audit
    7.5.4   System-based audit
    7.5.5   Risk-based audit
    7.5.6   Performance audit
    7.5.7   Best value audit or value-for-money (VFM) audit
    7.5.8   Post-completion audit
    7.5.9   Environmental audit
    7.5.10 Management audit.

 Each of the above audit types has a specific purpose or focus and knowledge of their definition and purpose is of key importance to the management accountant. The participant is strongly advised to study this section carefully and to be able to distinguish between different types of audit. The general principles of auditing, insofar as it effect this course, apply to all of the above auditing types.

7.6   From the definitions of internal audit (as detailed in the Learning System) it is apparent that the inclusion of an internal auditing process aids management in evaluating the effectiveness of risk management, control and governance processes.

7.7   In the light of increased pressure requiring boards of directors to comply with corporate governance legislation, the role of the internal audit, as an extension or aid to the board in meeting their commitments, has become more acute.

7.8   The scope of the internal audit should be such that it has an unrestricted access to all activities in the organisation. The internal auditor is expected to review and report on a wide range of issues including:

    7.8.1   Adequacy and effectiveness of systems;
    7.8.2   Compliance with policies, plans and procedures;
    7.8.3   Economical and efficient use of assets and related safeguards of loss;
    7.8.4   Suitability, accuracy, reliability and integrity of both financial and non-financial performance information;
    7.8.5   Integrity of processes and systems;
    7.8.6   Business unit suitability in terms of economical, efficient and effective operation;
    7.8.7   Adequacy of follow-up procedures;
    7.8.8   Effectiveness of corporate governance policies.

 It is important to note that the responsibility for the planning, implementation and execution of the structure, processes and operations lies with line management and the internal auditor has the responsibility for evaluating and reporting on the suitability, effectiveness and performance of the above elements.

Human nature, organisational politics, corporate and national culture, and power – distance relationships will all have a bearing on the independence of the internal auditor and the scope of influence and access that will be allowed.

7.9 Emphasis is placed, in this course, on the internal audit, systems-based auditing and risk-based internal auditing.

7.10 Risk-based audit extends the scope beyond financial issues into the broader internal control systems. Audit will pay attention to inherent risks, failure of controls, residual and audit risk. Figure 7.1 in the *Learning System* provides a useful diagram showing the components of risk-based audit.

7.11 Risk assessment in auditing will include:

7.11.1 Intuitive or judgemental assessment
7.11.2 Risk assessment matrix
7.11.3 Risk ranking.

7.12 Audit planning will include resourcing and time to conduct a survey for:

7.12.1 Review of previous internal audit reports and files;
7.12.2 Consideration of changes in the business environment;
7.12.3 Review of external auditors and other control processes;
7.12.4 Obtaining input from an local managers;
7.12.5 Risks identification;
7.12.6 Establishment of audit objectives.

7.13 The plan will set out:

7.13.1 Terms of reference of the audit
7.13.2 Description of the systems and processes
7.13.3 Risks that need special attention
7.13.4 Scope of the work to be carried out
7.13.5 Milestones
7.13.6 Reporting and review procedure
7.13.7 Program and techniques to be applied
7.13.8 Resourcing requirements.

7.14 The internal auditor will deploy methods and models including walk -through, compliance and substantive tests. This will involve techniques such as statistical sampling, analytic review using ratio analysis, non-financial performance analysis and benchmarking. Other methods used by internal auditors include physical inspection, corroboration, recalculation, surveys, narratives, flowcharts and internal control questionnaires.

7.15 Ethical conduct of an internal auditor is founded in the following principles:

7.15.1 Integrity
7.15.2 Objectivity
7.15.3 Professional competence and due care
7.15.4 Confidentiality
7.15.5 Professional behaviour

It is very important to note that CIMA Members are required to comply with the ethical guidelines that are published in Chartered Institute of Management Accountants (2006).

7.16 A key area for consideration is the existence of conflicts of interest. CIMA members are required to manage these conflicts and should:

7.16.1 Follow the organization's grievance policies;

7.16.2 Escalate the issue through successive levels of management, always with the member's superior's knowledge;

7.16.3 Consult an objective adviser or professional body;

7.16.4 When all else fails, the member may have no recourse but to resign and report the matter to the organisation.

7.17 The Learning System provides an extensive list of questions that enable judgement of the effectiveness of the internal audit.

Theory Revision Questions

The questions in this section are intended to assist you with learning the relevant concepts relating to internal audit. It is important to memorise and learn these concepts and tools for later recall in the examination. After studying this section, you should attempt the questions in Sections 2 and 3. Questions in Sections 2 and 3 enable you to apply these concepts and tools in composite business problem scenarios. The examination is designed around composite scenario problem solving type questions and Sections 2 and 3 have informed mainly on past exam papers as examples for you to prepare appropriately.

7.1 Defined the term "audit".

7.2 Differentiate between a financial audit and a compliance audit.

7.3 What it is the purpose of a best-value audit?

7.4 How does the internal audit differ from an external (or financial) audit?

7.5 Discuss factors that could have a bearing on the validity and quality of an internal audit.

7.6 What role does the scope of an internal audit play in its validity?

7.7 List the elements of a 'system-based' audit.

7.8 What are the objectives of risk-based auditing?

7.9 List the characteristics and internal audit approach for different levels of risk maturity.

7.10 Differentiate between *inherent risks* and *residual risk*.

7.11 What factors should be included in a risk assessment matrix?

7.12 What measures can be taken against risk?

7.13 What should an audit plan be comprised of?

7.14 List ten techniques used in internal auditing.

7.15 Describe three test techniques applied in auditing.

7.16 What documents would a set of standardised audit working papers include?

7.17 What should the Head of internal audit expect to report to the audit committee of the board?

7.18 List the fundamental principles that relate to the work of CIMA members.

7.19 What process should a CIMA member follow in the face of a sustained conflict of interest?

7.20 List some of the questions that could assist in judging the effectiveness of an internal audit.

✓ Theory Revision Solutions

7.1 *Audit is a systematic examination of the activities and status of an entity, based primarily on investigation and analysis of its systems, controls and records* (CIMA *Official Terminology*).

7.2 *A financial audit* is typically conducted by external auditors with a view to express an opinion on whether the financial statements present a "true and fair view" and comply with applicable accounting standards.

A compliance audit is an audit of specific activities in order to determine whether performance is in conformity with a predetermined contractual, regulatory or statutory requirement (CIMA *Official Terminology*).

7.3 Best-value audits enable an organisation (predominantly organisations not for gain including the public sector) to evaluate the economy, efficiency and effectiveness of operations in the absence of profit measures.

7.4 The objective of an internal audit is: "*to assist members of the organisation in the effective discharge of their responsibilities*" (CIMA *Official Terminology*).

By contrast, the financial audit is directed at meeting needs of external stakeholders and shareholders by requiring a registered professional to express his opinion as to the 'true and fair' presentation of the company's performance and position as represented in the financial statements.

7.5 The validity and quality of an internal audit is heavily dependent upon the independence and objectivity of the internal auditor. Organisational culture, national culture, power–distance relationships, organisational politics, organisational size and the board's attitude towards the internal audit function all have a pivotal role to play in the objectivity, access, output and prominence accorded to their role.

The internal audit function, to be truly effective, requires an unrestricted access to all activities in the organisation.

7.6 There is a fine line between the role of the internal auditor and the authority and responsibility of line management. Care has to be taken to ensure that an internal audit is properly scoped and that authority and access is given to the auditor to review and report on the following:

- The adequacy and effectiveness of systems of financial, operational and management control;
- The extent of compliance with, and the effect of policies, plans and procedures;
- Safety from loss and economy and efficiency of assets;
- The integrity of processes and systems;
- The suitability of business units' structures and organisation for carrying out its functions economically, efficiently and effectively;
- Follow-up and corrective action weaknesses identified;
- Adequacy and compliance of corporate governance arrangements.

The scope of internal audit is often curtailed with the resultant reduction in objective, reliability and completeness of the process.

7.7   A system-based audit should comprise the following:

- Identification of the objective of the system or process;
- Identification of the prescribed procedures to achieve the system objective and corporate objectives;
- Identification of risks in relation to the achievement of objectives;
- Identification of the management methodology established to determine and manage the risks;
- Evaluates whether the controls in place are appropriate;
- Tests to determine whether the controls are operating effectively in practice;
- Reports covering the findings and monitoring of the implementation of agreed recommendations.

7.8   The objectives of risk-based internal auditing are:

- To determine whether the risk management processes are operating as intended;
- The risk management processes are part of a sound design;
- That risk treatment/responses to risks are adequate and effective in reducing those risks to a level acceptable to the board;
- Effective control signed place to mitigate those risks of which management wishes to-treat.

7.9

Risk maturity	Key characteristics	Internal audit approach
Risk Naive	No formal approach developed for risk management	Promotes risk management and rely on audit risk assessment
Risk Aware	Scattered silo-based approach to risk management	Promote enterprise-wide approach to risk management and rely on audit risk assessment
Risk Defined	Strategy and policies in place and communicated. Risk appetite defined.	Facilitate risk management and/or liaise with risk management and use management assessment of risk where appropriate.
Risk Managed	Enterprise-wide approach to risk management developed and communicated.	Ordered risk management processes and use management assessment of risk as appropriate.
Risk Enabled	Risk management and internal control for the embedded into the operations.	Audit risk management processes and use assessment management of the risk as appropriate.

Source: Institute of Internal Auditors (2003), Risk Based Internal Auditing from Table 7.1 in the *Learning System*.

7.10   *Inherent risks* are those risks that follow from the nature of the business and its environment in which it operates while *residual risk* is that risk which remains after controls have been implemented. Residual risk comprises those risks that are not covered by controls and treatment.

7.11   A risk assessment matrix should comprise of the following factors:

- Transaction volume
- Impact on business continuity
- Adequacy of existing controls
- Weather systems are new or long-established
- Quality and experience of staff and management
- Susceptibility to fraud.

7.12   Measures or treatment that can be taken against risk are:

- Transferring the risk through insurance, hedging, use of partners, joint ventures, networks and sharing;
- Reduce the likelihood of risk by the introduction of controls;
- Reducing exposure to risk by avoiding or eliminating activities that are risky generating and/or through the introduction of controls;
- Detecting occurrences through alerts and feedback mechanisms;
- Recovering from occurrences through the provision of redundancy and contingency planning.

7.13   The audit plan should be comprised of the following:

- The terms of reference for the audit;
- Description of the system or process to be audited; identifying its boundaries and connections to other systems and processes;
- Risks that need special attention;
- Scope of work to be carried out, identifying any areas not to be audited;
- Milestone dates for completion and resources allocated to the audit;
- Reporting and review procedure;
- Audit program and techniques to be applied;
- Audit staff allocated to the assignment.

7.14   Techniques used in internal auditing include:

1 Statistical sampling
2 Ratio analysis
3 Benchmarking
4 Physical inspection
5 Corroboration
6 Re-calculation and reconciliation
7 Surveys and questionnaires
8 Narrative descriptions of processes or systems
9 Flowcharting
10 Testing.

7.15   Three test techniques applied in auditing are:

1 *Walk-through tests* which follow several transactions through the system from their origin to the end of the process.
2 *Compliance tests* audit of control which determine whether system controls are operating as intended.
3 *Substantive tests* which aim to establish the validity of the outcome of transactions. These tests are deployed more extensively when compliance tests indicate weak controls or when fraud is suspected.

7.16 A standardized set of audit working papers should include:

- Scope and type of audit
- Report from previous audit and recommendations outstanding
- Timetable for the audit and resources allocated to the audit
- Work programs including analytical methods used
- Evidence collected from ratio analysis, benchmarking, narratives, flowcharts and testing
- Interpretation of the evidence and significant findings
- Conclusions
- Recommendations
- Final report.

7.17 The Head internal audit should expect to report to the Audit Committee of the Board as follows:

- Provide regular assessments of the adequacy and effectiveness of systems of the risk management and internal control processes;
- Report significant internal control issues and potential for improving risk management and control;
- Provide information on the status and results of the annual order to plan and the adequacy of resources for internal audit.

7.18 The fundamental principles that relate to the work of CIMA members are:

- Integrity
- Objectivity
- Professional competence and due care
- Confidentiality
- Professional behaviour
- Technical standards.

The participant is required to know the contents of the latest 2006 Code of Ethics for Professional Accountants which is available from CIMA and is based on IFAC guidelines.

7.19 A CIMA member should escalate according to the following steps when faced with a sustained conflict of interests:

1 Follow the organisation's grievance policy;
2 Discuss the matter with the member's superior and successive levels of management always with the member's superior's knowledge;
3 Seek advice From an objective adviser or the professional body;
4 After exhausting all of the prior levels, the member may have no other option other than to resign and report the matter to the organisation.

7.20 The Institute of Internal Auditors (2003), *Appraising Internal* Audit lists 29 questions that assist in judging the effectiveness of internal audit.

The following ten questions were extracted from this list:

1 Has the purpose, authority and responsibility of the internal audit function been formally defined and approved by the audit committee?
2 Has any consulting activity carried out by internal audit detracted from the primary role?
3 Is internal audit capable of identifying the indicators of fraud?

4   Has the work of the internal audit considered all important business risks?

5   Has there been any significant control breakdown in areas that have been reviewed by internal audit?

6   Does internal audit undertake a program of continuous improvement?

7   Are internal audit practices benchmarked against best practice?

8   Does internal audit carry out its role in accordance with the IIA's International Standards for the Professional Practice of Internal Auditing?

9   Can internal audit respond quickly to organisational change?

10 Does internal audit have the necessary resources and access to information to enable it to carry out its role?

The participant should be familiar with the range of questions for judging audit effectiveness which are set out in detail in the CIMA *Learning System*.

Information Systems and Systems Development

Information Systems and Systems Development

8

LEARNING OUTCOMES

After completing this chapter in the CIMA *Learning System* you should be able to

- evaluate and advise managers on the development of IM, IS and IT strategies that support management and internal control requirements;
- identify and evaluate IS/IT systems appropriate to an organisation's needs for operational and control information;
- evaluate benefits and risks in the structuring and organisation of the IS/IT function and its integration with the rest of the business;
- evaluate and recommend improvements to the control of information systems.

Theory Highlights from CIMA Official Study System

8.1 Information is the result of making data usable for decision-making. Organisations require information to manage and control the processes.

8.2 With the advent of computerisation, information management and dissemination has been substantially enhanced in terms of timeliness, accuracy, completeness and the speed with which large volumes of data can be managed and transformed in an automated fashion.

8.3 IM/IS/IT

It is very important for the participant to understand the relationship between information management, information systems and information technology. In the management accounting context, the role of information technology in providing an efficient formal system for data collection, management, control and communication continues to grow exponentially throughout all industries. The management accountant will be involved in programmes that integrate all facets of the organisations that extend way beyond the financial realm. These programmes are built on information systems that have varying degrees of reliability, integrity and performance. These systems across company, country and continent borders that not only provide the globalisation benefit of instant information anywhere in the world but simultaneously exposes the corporation's data and information to the ravages of industrial espionage and related crimes.

The quality, reliability and timious receipt of relevant information is the domain of the corporations information system. It is at this level that the data and information contained within the IT programmes are integrated with non-IT programme based data and information to complete the picture. The participant is urged to explore and understand the concepts of controllable systems (sometimes referred to as hard systems) and those that are more difficult to control (sometimes referred to as soft systems). The machine/human interface is one of these difficult to control areas where it is neither practical nor possible to control all of the variables.

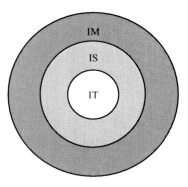

8.4 With globalisation, crumbling national boundaries in terms of business and trade, the ease with which information can be shared and transferred globally via the Internet, organisations are facing ever-increasing opportunities and challenges in the realm of information systems strategy.

8.5 Contemporary knowledge management strategies elevate the debate beyond information management; encompassing formalised methodologies to convert implicit knowledge to explicit knowledge whenever possible; to manage the collection, dissemination and sharing of knowledge on a scale not possible prior to the development of mineable accessible databases.

8.6 Along with the cost-benefit debate of collecting, processing, analysing and dissemination of information, the organisation is now faced with ever-increasing demand for hardware and software to deal with the accelerating flow of data, information and knowledge.

8.7 This course focuses primarily on contemporary information management systems. A large proportion of the focus remains periodic reporting for management including transactions, exception and summarised periodic results. Online, real-time dashboards or briefing books provide managers with key summary information, often in graphical form, to aid with the need for focused attention on critical issues.

8.8   Information systems are concerned with transaction processing, management information, enterprise resource planning, strategic enterprise management, decision support and expert systems. Depending upon the type of organisation, varying degrees of complexity and integration are required. Comprehensive integrated enterprise resource planning systems that extend to decision support, executive information and functional extensions including customer and supplier/supply chain management are available and are becoming accessible even to medium-sized enterprises.

8.9   TCP/IP Technology integrates the movement and sharing of data, images, audio files and real-time video and audio communication over the Internet.

8.10   Internet and extranet technology has enhanced the capability of inter-organisational commerce (E-commerce) and has transformed the banking industry into a global high speed superpower.

8.11   The pace of change, and the escalating level of complexity and scope of IT systems, has sustained the tendency for organisations to outsource this function in whole or in part. Key advantages include greater access to scarce resources and skill, cost savings, improved quality and flexibility to keep up with changing technologies. On the other hand, disadvantages of outsourcing include difficulty in establishing clear service level agreements, risk of unsatisfactory quality and service, higher exposure to information leakage to competitors and hidden complexities and expense relating to unchanged overhead burdens, changeover difficulties and management issues relating to supervision of the outsourced supplier.

8.12   In many organisations, IS development is a key strategic focus requiring organisations to develop competencies in systems design, development and control. This extends the requirement for organisations auditing capabilities to include systems development auditing.

8.13   If not outsourced, the organisation will require skill and competency in terms of systems implementation, post-implementation review and continual improvement projects capability.

8.14   The Information Technology Infrastructure Library (ITIL) is an internationally accepted best practice model that guides business users through the planning, delivery and management of quality IT services. The Service Support processes and goals of the ITIL are:

      8.13.1   Configuration management
      8.13.2   Incident management
      8.13.3   Change management
      8.13.4   Problem management
      8.13.5   Release management.

8.15   The ITIL Service Delivery processes and goals are:

      8.14.1   Service level management
      8.14.2   Availability management
      8.14.3   Capability management
      8.14.4   IT services continuity management
      8.14.5   Financial management.

8.16   No organisation can manage and control risk without robust security and integrity management of, and redundancy and contingency infrastructure surrounding, IT systems. The potential for data and information security breaches, hacking, data tampering and the effects of errors of omission and commission by employees renders organisations vulnerable. As a result, ever increasing demand is being placed upon management accountants, auditors and IT professionals to improve and refine financial, non-financial, quantitative and qualitative systems in a highly integrated environment.

Theory Revision Questions

 The questions in this section are intended to assist you with learning the relevant concepts relating to information systems. It is important to memorise and learn these concepts and tools for later recall in the examination. After studying this section, you should attempt the questions in Sections 2 and 3. Questions in Sections 2 and 3 enable you to apply these concepts and tools in composite business problem scenarios. The examination is designed around composite scenario problem solving type questions and Sections 2 and 3 have informed mainly on past exam papers as examples for you to prepare appropriately.

8.1   What is information?

8.2   What is an information system?

8.3   Name three organisational strategies relating to information.

8.4   Distinguish between electronic point-of-sale (EPOS) and Internet purchasing and discuss the advantages of each of these technologies to the organisation.

8.5   Name several methods of data collection.

8.6   Discuss four methods of presenting information to management.

8.7   Distinguish between transaction processing systems and management information systems.

8.8   Distinguish between enterprise resource planning systems and strategic enterprise management.

8.9   Discuss the roles of decision support systems (DSS) and executive information systems (EIS).

8.10   What roles do expert systems play in an organisation?

8.11   Distinguish between intranets and extranets and list three applications for each.

8.12   What are the major benefits of E-commerce to the organisation?

8.13   List the major advantages and disadvantages of IS outsourcing.

8.14   List the key elements of IS project management.

8.15   List the stages of the Systems Development Life Cycle.

8.16   Describe the key controls of each of the SDLC stages.

8.17   What is the role of internal audit in relation to the development of a new IS system?

8.18   What are the expected outcomes of a post-implementation review?

8.19   What are the functions of an information center?

8.20   What service and support can business organisations expect from the Information Technology Infrastructure Library?

✓ Theory Revision Solutions

8.1 Information is an assembly of raw data that has been converted into a form that informs a user about the data.

8.2 Information system is a system that collects data and transforms it into information and presents it, usually in summarised form, for management.

8.3 Organisations deploy the following three information strategies:

1 *Information systems strategy* focused on the long-term systems required to host information technologies;
2 *Information technology strategy* defines specific information technologies necessary to support the business strategy of the organisation;
3 *Information management strategy* is concerned with methods by which data is stored, converted into information and made available for access.

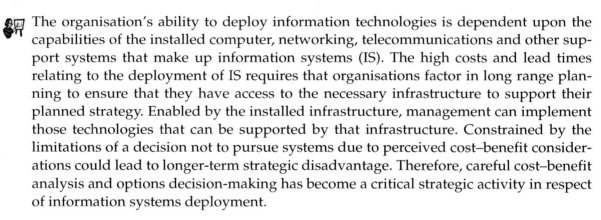 The organisation's ability to deploy information technologies is dependent upon the capabilities of the installed computer, networking, telecommunications and other support systems that make up information systems (IS). The high costs and lead times relating to the deployment of IS requires that organisations factor in long range planning to ensure that they have access to the necessary infrastructure to support their planned strategy. Enabled by the installed infrastructure, management can implement those technologies that can be supported by that infrastructure. Constrained by the limitations of a decision not to pursue systems due to perceived cost–benefit considerations could lead to longer-term strategic disadvantage. Therefore, careful cost–benefit analysis and options decision-making has become a critical strategic activity in respect of information systems deployment.

These decisions have broad ranging implications for information management strategy. A broad range of advantages can be gained from information technology deployment including automation, integration and sharing benefits, dissemination across domestic and global boundaries and standardisation across the organisation. Risks include a loss of control over ownership and access to information, potential tampering and distortion that could affect (parts of or) the entire organisation, unintended uses and outcomes.

A potential cascade of implications resulting from long range board decisions not to invest in IS that, in turn, inhibits the deployment of appropriate information technology that may be critical to the achievement of the organisation strategic goals and/or the management of activities and information critical to achieving the objectives of the strategy of the organization.

8.4 EPOS is an 'in-store' technology that uses barcodes to price goods that, amongst others, enables the organisation to reduce inventory, identify margins by linking the sales price to cost of goods sold, to manage receipts, holding and disposal strategies and manage information regarding customer purchase patterns.
Internet purchasing, on the other hand, enables customers to carry out the doctor processing for themselves remotely from the retailer enabling the retailer to reduce staff, reduce cost of retail space, improved efficiency through automation and trade with clients over a broader geographical spread.

8.5 Methods of data collection include:

1 Electronic point of sale (EPOS)
2 Electronic funds transfer at point of sale (EFTPOS)
3 Loyalty cards
4 Internet purchasing
5 Electronic data interchange (EDI)
6 Document imaging.

8.6 Four methods of presenting management information include:

1 *Transaction reports*: Detailed reports of transactions conducted over a period;
2 *Exception reports*: Lists exceptions to predetermined rules;
3 Summarized periodic reports: reports produced at regular intervals;
4 *Briefing-book*: Typically comprised of one-page summaries of key financial or non-financial information.

Contemporary trends include online, real-time dashboards and alerts that enable managers to react and control key aspects of the business with reduced delays resulting in increased successes and performance.

8.7 *Transaction processing systems* collect source data about each business transaction while *management information systems* convert raw data into usable form and disseminate this information to managers and staff.

8.8 Enterprise resource planning systems help to integrate data flow and access to information from sources throughout the company. This integrated data is then disseminated to users in the organization in accordance with their needs.

Strategic enterprise management systems extended the use of collected data for analysis using computer-based analytical tools and techniques to provide information needed for strategic management decision-making.

8.9 Decision support systems generally contain data analysis models that enable managers to simulate different options. Executive information systems, on the other hand, provide managers with 'drill-down' facilities, giving them access, often in summarised form, to key information based upon actual organisation transactions and data.

8.10 Expert systems store data gained from experts and are often deployed to automate decision-making or provide parameter-driven boundaries within which decisions can be taken.

8.11 Intranets are in-house versions of the Internet, operated by a single organisation. Extranets are systems that link the intranets of related organisations.

Applications for intranets include:

• Telephone lists
• Procedure manuals
• Reference materials (and many more).

Extranets include applications that provide mutual benefit to the organisations and include:

• Price information
• Delivery schedules
• Stock availability (and many more).

8.12 The major benefits of E-commerce to an organisation include:

- Expanding access to a greater/global marketplace;
- Reduction in transaction costs;
- Extending the reach of related activities including public relations, information dissemination and marketing.

8.13 The major advantages of IS outsourcing include:

- More accurate prediction of costs
- Using only the requisite amount of capacity necessary
- Improved to highly skilled specialists
- Economies of scale access to it through the outsource service provider
- Reduced burden on managing specialist staff
- Improved quality and service.

The major disadvantages of IS outsourcing include:

- Complications with service level agreements that clearly delineate the responsibilities of each party;
- Some loss of flexibility due to the constraints of the contract with the outsource supplier;
- Risk of unsatisfactory quality and service or even failure of the supplier;
- Short-term cost-savings focus at the expense of long-term strategy considerations;
- Sustained overhead burden in addition to outsourcing costs;
- Changeover management complexities;
- Potential management complications with outsource supplier;

8.14 The key elements of IS project management are:

- Project planning and definition
- Senior management commitment
- Project organisation including roles and responsibilities of the steering committee, project board and project manager
- Resource planning and allocation
- Quality control and progress monitoring
- Risk management
- Systems design and approval
- Systems testing and implementation
- User participation and involvement
- Communication and coordination
- User education and training.

8.15 The Systems Development Life Cycle comprises the following stages:

- Feasibility study
- Systems analysis
- Systems design
- Implementation
- Systems operation and maintenance.

8.16 The key controls at each of the SDLC stages are:

- *Feasibility study stage*: At this stage there should be clear understanding of objectives of the system, deliverables, its cost and time to completion.
- *Systems analysis stage*: At this stage, a high level of expertise and information is required of the problem in order to establish a detailed specification for the system.
- *Systems design stage*: During the design stage, controls are required to ensure that the conversion process meets specification in terms of security, data storage, input layouts, file structure, reports and interfaces with other systems. Comprehensive testing should be conducted on the system and audit is should review the specification, flowcharts, test data and operating instructions.
- *Implementation stage*: Key controls at this stage are verification of staffing competency and supervision.
- *Systems operation and maintenance stage*: Controls include system stability verification, input-conversion-output congruency, staffing competence and systems uptime monitoring.

8.17 The role of internal audit in relation to the development of a new IS system includes:

- Ensure that risks are adequately addressed
- Testing input-conversion-output congruency of financial and non-financial information
- Ensure that an audit trail is present
- Review the scope for possible fraud.

8.18 The expected outcomes of a post-implementation review are:

- The new system satisfies users' needs
- System performance meets the system specification
- Actual costs are within budgeted project costs
- Variations and improvements identified in the development process have been incorporated
- Further recommendations for improvement to the system.

8.19 The functions of an information centre include:

- User problem solving (often through the means of a helpdesk)
- Integration and purchase of hardware and software
- Advice on application development
- Monitoring and maintenance of network system
- Maintaining corporate databases or data warehouses
- System maintenance and testing
- Maintaining IT security.

8.20 Business organisations can expect the following support and service from the ITIL:

- *Configuration management*: To identify, record and report on all IT components.
- *Incident management*: To restore normal service operations as quickly as possible and minimise the adverse impact on business operations.
- *Change management*: To ensure that standardised methods and procedures are used for efficient and prompt handling of all changes to minimise the impact of change-related incidents and improve day-to-day operations.
- *Problem management*: To minimise the adverse impact of incidents and problems on the business that are caused by errors in the IT infrastructure.
- *Release management*: To ensure that both technical and non-technical attributes of a release are considered together.

Information Systems
Control and Auditing

Information Systems Control and Auditing

9

LEARNING OUTCOMES

After completing this chapter in the CIMA *Learning System* you should be able to

- explain the importance of management review of controls;
- evaluate the process of internal audit;
- produce a plan for the audit of various organisational activities including management, accounting and information systems;
- analyse problems associated with the audit of activities and systems, and recommend action to avoid or solve those problems;
- recommend action to improve the efficiency, effectiveness and control of activities;
- evaluate and recommend improvements to the control of information systems;
- evaluate specific problems and opportunities associated with the audit and control of systems which use information technology.

Theory Highlights from CIMA Official Study System

9.1 IT systems, as we have seen in the previous chapter, have become a critical strategic competitive tool in the information/globalisation age. As with other business processes, management has to maintain control over its various facets with particular emphasis upon risk management. In order to measure and monitor risk, the board, line management, information systems experts and auditors have to devote resources and attention to the management and monitoring of IT in addition to the remaining financial and non-financial elements of the business.

9.2 Because the IT and enterprise information systems are inextricably bound to the IS system, modern control and management systems tend to be comprehensive and integrated. CobiT, SAC, eSAC and COSO number among the many integrated control models in use.

9.3 Control strategies cover security, integrity and contingencies. These areas are best protected by predictive controls or preventative controls. If those are not available then one has to resort to detective controls and corrective controls.

9.4 These controls can be further categorised as being general, application, software and network control focused. General controls comprise controls over personnel, access, facility and business continuity. Application controls apply to input, processing and output. Software controls prevent using unauthorised copies of software and breaching copyright. Network controls prevent hacking, viruses, and other external attacks.

9.5 In order to undertake auditing of a computer system, specialised skills are required and a thorough understanding of the system is mandatory. Technological developments have seen the evolution of Computer Assisted Audit Techniques (CAATs) that enable automated review of system controls and data. More advanced systems include embedded audit facilities that enable continuous audit review of data, its processing and interrogation, with parallel access to the system for audit purposes.

Theory Revision Questions

 The questions in this section are intended to assist you with learning the relevant concepts relating to IS control and audit. It is important to memorise and learn these concepts and tools for later recall in the examination. After studying this section, you should attempt the questions in Sections 2 and 3. Questions in Sections 2 and 3 enable you to apply these concepts and tools in composite business problem scenarios. The examination is designed around composite scenario problem solving type questions and Sections 2 and 3 have informed mainly on past exam papers as examples for you to prepare appropriately.

9.1   Identify some of the features necessary for information security.

9.2   What are the major risks faced by organizations in relation to electronic commerce?

9.3   Compare the three systems control models: CobiT, eSAC and COSO.

9.4   Name the three broad categories of systems controls.

9.5   Draw a distinction between predictive and preventative controls.

9.6   What logical access controls can be applied to regulate unauthorised access to data?

9.7   List the steps necessary for business continuity planning.

9.8   Identify the main Application controls.

9.9   List the main risks for which network controls are imperative.

9.10   Explain the function of Firewalls in network controls.

9.11   How can Internet payment transactions be protected?

9.12   Describe three forms of hacking.

9.13   What additional measures can be added to provide increased security against hacking?

9.14   List the basic principles of computer system auditing.

9.15   Discuss the main techniques used to review system controls.

9.16   What is the function of audit interrogation software?

9.17   What is the purpose of a SCARF file?

9.18   What is the function of simulation in the context of data review techniques?

9.19   What is the benefit of systems maintenance auditing?

9.20   What are the implications of software piracy for a user organization?

✅ Theory Revision Solutions

9.1 The BS 7799 (ISO 17799) information system security best practice checklist comprises:

- Security policy
- Security organization
- Asset classification and control
- Personnel security
- Physical and environmental security
- Computer and network management
- Systems access controls
- Systems development and maintenance
- Business continuity and disaster recovery
- Compliance.

9.2 eSAC defines e-commerce risks as follows:

- Fraud
- Errors of omission and commission
- Business interruptions
- Inefficient use of resources
- Ineffective use of resources.

9.3 The comparison between the three models is as follows:

CobiT views internal controls as a process that includes policies, procedures, practices and organisational structures that support business processes and objectives.

eSAC emphasises internal control as a system, a set of functions, sub-systems, people and the interrelationship between all of those.

The COSO model emphasises internal control as a process which is integrated with business activities.

9.4 Systems controls include security, integrity and contingency controls.

9.5 Predictive controls identify likely problems/risks and introduce appropriate controls. Preventative controls minimise the possibility of a risk occurring.

9.6 The following logical access controls can be applied to regulate unauthorised access to data:

- Regular changes to passwords
- Password formats including minimum length requirements and alphanumeric character combinations
- Prevention of screen display of password during typing
- Encryption
- Lock-out after multiple unsuccessful log-in attempts
- Time-outs after disuse for a predetermined period
- Logging of access.

9.7 Business continuity planning includes:

- Making a risk assessment
- Developing a contingency it plan to address those risks
- The roles and responsibility of key individuals should be defined
- Backup facilities for all data

- Alternative sites for data processing established
- Equipment providers identified
- Stuffing and succession planning
- Processes necessary to restore business-critical information to enable the organisation to continue operating;
- Determine the time involved to restore computer systems and business-critical information.

9.8   Application controls include input controls, processing controls and output controls. Input controls involve authorisation of transactions prior to data entry, password and access control, data entry screens prescribing the format for data entry online verification codes, limits, reasonableness checks and adjustment controls.

Processing controls include standardization, control totals and balancing techniques.

Output controls include transaction listing, exception reports, forms control, suspense accounts and distribution lists.

9.9   The main risks for which network controls are imperative are:

- Hacking via the Internet
- Computer virus or worm
- Electronic eavesdropping into confidential information
- Credit card payments via the Internet rejected fraudulently
- Accidental or deliberate alteration of data transferred over the network
- Human error of omission or commission
- Computer system malfunction
- Natural disasters.

9.10   Firewalls are a combination of hardware and software that are located between that set of the organisation's computer system requiring screening and those accessible from outside. Firewalls enable an organisation to restrict access to selected systems and data through a single gateway, enabling password controlled access to defined users.

9.11   Transactions, for example Internet payments, are protected using a process of data encryption. Encryption is a process whereby data is converted into a non-readable format before transmission and then re-converted after transmission.

9.12   Hacking could comprise the following three forms:

- Traffic escalation that overloads a website resulting in it going offline;
- Access obtained through password security breach;
- Insertion of viruses.

9.13   Methods that can be deployed to provide additional security against hacking are:

- Vulnerability testing through deliberate attempts to breach security;
- Regular monitoring, alerts and vigilance of staff to detect intrusion;
- Virus scanning of all emails received.

9.14   The basic principles of auditing a computer system are:

- Understanding the system
- Identifying how the system can be tested
- Reviewing security
- Data encryption validation
- Information accuracy generated by the system

- Validation of transaction and amendment authorization
- Transaction acknowledgement/confirmation systems
- Data validity checking
- Backup of data files on a regular basis
- Recovery procedures validation.

9.15 The main techniques used to review system controls are:

- *Test data.* A set of data that is processed by a computer and compared with expected results based upon manual processing;
- *Embedded audit facilities.* Functionality incorporated into the system that allows for continuous audit review of data and its processing. The verification of embedded audit facilities is executed by introducing a known false entry. Other examples of embedded audit facilities are code comparison programs and logical path analysis programs.

9.16 Audit interrogation software enables auditors to:

- Extract data from files for further audit work
- Interrogate computer files and extract required information
- Perform statistical analysis quickly and accurately
- Verify management reports with system data
- Detect items that are not system rule compliant.

9.17 A SCARF (Systems Control And Review File) is used to collect selected data items extracted from financial records to enable thei95r investigation by an auditor at a later time.

9.18 Simulation, as a data review technique, involves the preparation of a separate program that simulates the operation of the organisation's real system.

9.19 Systems maintenance auditing verifies that change control, documentation and authorisation procedures have been followed.

9.20 User organisations deploying pirated software face the following disadvantages:

- Higher propensity for failure
- Absence of warranties and support
- Increased risk of viruses and negative impacts on systems
- Significant exposure to financial penalties and/or criminal prosecution
- Reputation risk.

Fraud

Fraud

10

Theory Highlights from CIMA Official Study System

 Fraud is a subset of the risks facing corporations that require management control. The participant should integrate learning in this chapter with the risk management theory, practice and processes that make up the majority of the learning of this module. The focus of this chapter is to direct the participant's learning towards those regulations, statutes, policies, procedures and controls that specifically apply to fraud. Ideally, fraud should be prevented but, in the real world, we have to accept that systems will not be perfect and that as many smart people may be involved in the process of beating the system as there are designing and developing systems. The expansion of information systems to include intelligence and the growth of crime prevention services to corporations is evidence of the growing sophistication and complexity involved in this area.

10.1   Fraud represents one of the highest incidence of white collar crime. Recent high-profile corporate failures, particularly those in the USA, have brought about the introduction by governments of corporate governance legislation that is enforcing upon boards of directors to assume responsibility that, in some cases, can result in personal criminal prosecution and/or substantial personal and corporate financial penalties.

10.2   The Sarbanes-Oxley statute in the USA is a prominent corporate governance measure that aim to provide safeguards against fraudulent behaviour in relation to financial reporting by senior executives.

10.3   Internally, management has the responsibility of providing controls to guard against crimes committed by or against customers, employees, financial institutions, and suppliers, or against the government and whether carried out locally or internationally.

10.4   For fraud to be perpetrated, dishonesty, opportunity and motive must pre-exist. Management has the responsibility of monitoring for and implementing controls to counter or mitigate the effects that fraud could have upon the organisation and its stakeholders.

10.5   Factors that play a determining role in fraud prevention are the establishment of an anti-fraud culture, cultivating risk awareness, implementing and supporting whistle blowing and the installation of sound internal controls.

10.6   It is important for management of organisations to be aware that external auditors do not have the responsibility for detecting fraud. Management has the task of structuring, leading, culture creation and installation of systems and methods to identify and respond to fraud.

10.7   Computer systems create an additional avenue through which fraud can be perpetrated and often provides a vehicle where fraud detection is more difficult to detect.

10.8   Management fraud constitutes a high proportion of corporate frauds. Their detection is made more difficult due to their position of power and their influence over others fortunes that renders whistle blowing ineffective.

10.9   Organised crime and syndicated fraud has become an even greater threat due to the increased volume of international trade and globalisation.

10.10   Fraud management strategy is a critical component of corporate risk management. In addition to implementing detection and monitoring systems and procedures, organisations act proactively by participating in industry and national crime prevention structures that enable them to leverage specialist skills including forensic, investigative and analysis techniques that are normally beyond the scope of commercial operations.

Theory Revision Questions

The questions in this section are intended to assist you with learning the relevant concepts relating to fraud. It is important to memorise and learn these concepts and tools for later recall in the examination. After studying this section, you should attempt the questions in Sections 2 and 3. Questions in Sections 2 and 3 enable you to apply these concepts and tools in composite business problem scenarios. The examination is designed around composite scenario problem solving type questions and Sections 2 and 3 have informed mainly on past exam papers as examples for you to prepare appropriately.

10.1   How is fraud defined?

10.2   Name the three prerequisites for fraud to occur.

10.3   What techniques can be deployed to counter dishonesty?

10.4   What measures can an organisation deploy to limit opportunity for fraud?

10.5   How can organisations manage motive?

10.6   List warning signs that may indicate the presence of fraud risk.

10.7   How can an organisation achieve fraud prevention?

10.8   Developing an anti-fraud culture is acknowledged as a sound contributor to fraud risk management. What should management focus on in order to develop an anti-fraud culture?

10.9   How can risk awareness be cultivated with employees?

10.10   Why are employees reluctant to blow the whistle on fraud?

10.11   How should organisations respond to fraud?

10.12   What particular set of controls should be deployed to counter computer fraud?

10.13   Management fraud has led to the collapse of many organisations. What specific indicators could alert the management accountant of the possibility of management fraud being present?

10.14   What is the impact of identity fraud on the individual and the organisation?

10.15   List three other forms of fraud that organisations should be vigilant for.

Theory Revision Solutions

10.1 Fraud can be defined as that conduct that results in someone obtaining an advantage, avoiding an obligation or causing a loss to another party dishonestly.

10.2 The three prerequisites necessary for fraud to be perpetrated are:

1 Dishonesty
2 Opportunity
3 Motive.

10.3 Techniques that can be deployed to counter dishonesty include:

- Pre-employment checks on all new staff
- Lifestyle monitoring of staff
- Severe discipline for offenders
- Proactive and effective moral leadership.

 The New York Police Department pursued a policy of prosecuting even the most minor of offences and, over a reasonably short time frame, found that all crime levels showed a declining tendency. This approach has subsequently been implemented in many other parts of the world with similar success profiles. Where organisations adopt a firm approach to deviant behaviour, however small, they will build knowledge and expertise in the handling of crime and fraud.

Corporations are implementing knowledge management systems to enable their processes. On growing aspect is corporate intelligence which places the corporation on a learning process. Through collaborative arrangements with other corporations, national and international security organisations, global corporations are developing measures, systems, organisations and strategies to counter the effects of international fraud.

To effectively manage fraud within the organisation it is necessary to configure controls, policies, procedures and develop a culture of intolerance of dishonesty and criminality so that when incidents occur everyone knows how to act and react with the expectation of management and leadership support and attitude. To this end, the management accountant can play a pivotal role in ensuring the design and maintenance of systems, policies and procedures that can be preventative of fraud.

10.4 The measures an organisation can deploy to limit opportunity for fraud include:

- Separation of duties where possible
- Controls over inputs
- Controls over processing
- Controls over outputs
- Physical security of assets
- Job and duty rotation
- Routine auditing
- Enforcing leave to be taken regularly
- Requiring control/authorisation by more than one individual.

10.5 Organizations can manage motives through:

- The establishment of good employment conditions
- A policy of instant dismissals where fraud is perpetrated

- Maintain sympathetic complaints procedures
- Provide support structures to alleviate employee distress
- Monitor behaviour and characteristics indicative of being motive indicators.

10.6 Warning signs that could indicate the presence of fraud risk include:

- Absence of anti-fraud culture
- Absence of sound system of internal controls
- Low levels of financial management expertise
- A history of legal or regulatory violations
- Strained relationships
- Lack of supervision staff
- Inadequate recruitment processes
- Redundancies
- Employee dissatisfaction
- Unusual staff behaviour
- Discrepancies between earnings and lifestyle
- Low salary levels of key staff
- Employees working unsocial hours unsupervised
- Lack of job segregation and independent checking of key transactions
- Poor management accountability and reporting
- Alteration of documents and records
- Photocopied documents replacing originals
- Missing authorisations
- Poor physical security of assets
- Poor access controls to physical assets and IT systems
- In adequacy of internal controls
- Poor documentation of internal controls
- Poor documentary support for transactions, especially credit notes
- Large cash transactions
- Management compensation highly dependent on meeting aggressive performance targets
- Significant pressure on management to obtain additional finance
- Extensive use of tax havens without clear business justification
- Complex transactions
- Complex legal ownership and/or organisational structure
- Rapid changes in profitability
- Existence of personal or corporate guarantees
- Highly competitive market conditions and decreasing profitability levels within the organisation
- The organisation operating in a declining business sector and facing possible business failure
- Rapid technological change which may increase potential for product obsolescence
- New accounting or regulatory requirements which could significantly alter reported results.

10.7 Fraud risk management prevention strategy includes:

- Anti-fraud culture
- Risk awareness
- Whistle blowing

- Sound internal control systems
- The fact that a fraud strategy exists also serves as a deterrent.

10.8 In order for management to develop an anti-fraud culture within the organisation, high ethical standards have to be cultivated. In order to cultivate these standards, management could follow the following guiding principles:

- Not acting in a way that could bring the organisation into disrepute;
- Acting with integrity towards colleagues, customers, suppliers and the public;
- Ensuring that business objectives are clearly stated and communicated:
- Ensuring that benefits are distributed fairly and impartially;
- Safeguarding the confidentiality of personal data;
- Complying with legal requirements.

10.9 Risk awareness can be cultivated through training, publicity of past events and ensuring that the possibility of fraud is kept top-of-mind with personnel in key positions.

10.10 Employees are reluctant to blow the whistle on fraud because of:

- Loyalties among workers
- Fear of the consequences
- Having unsubstantiated suspicions.

 The Public Interest Disclosure Act of 1999 provides limited protection for whistle-blowers and guidance to management. Until corporations enhance the policies within the organisation that strengthen the protection afforded to whistle-blowers that will encourage them to have confidence in making disclosures, management accountants will bear a disproportionate responsibility for preventing, detecting and controlling fraud.

10.11 Organisations should respond to fraud by:

- Applying internal disciplinary action in accordance with personnel policies;
- Pursuing a policy of civil litigation for recovery of the loss;
- Enforcing criminal prosecution through the police whenever possible.

10.12 The following particular set of controls could be deployed to counter computer fraud:

- Control and testing of program changes
- Physical security of computer systems
- Password controls
- Control over the issue of output forms including company orders, cheques and credits notes.

10.13 The management accountant should be vigilant for signs of management fraud by observing the following behaviour:

- Deliberate distortion of cut-off procedures to shift profits between years
- Capitalisation of expenses
- Under-provisions
- Over-valuation of inventory

- Manipulation of records to hide management incompetence
- Paying inflated prices to suppliers in return for bribes
- Employment of family members
- Charging personal expenses to the organisation.

10.14 The impact of identity fraud on the individual is that, once criminals have copied someone's identity, they can embark on criminal activity in that person's name with the knowledge that any follow-up investigations will not lead back to the criminals. This makes it difficult for organisations to know who they are really dealing with.

10.15 Organisations should be vigilant for the following additional forms of fraud:

- The so-called "419 fraud" where victims are asked to help move large sums of money with the promise of a substantial share of the cash in return
- High Yield Investment fraud and Prime Bank fraud
- Pyramid schemes.

Introduction to Risk Management and Derivatives

Introduction to Risk Management and Derivatives

11

LEARNING OUTCOMES

After completing this chapter in the CIMA *Learning System* you should be able to

- interpret the risks facing an organisation that arise from movements in interest rates;
- appreciate the purpose and functions of a treasury department;
- understand the different reasons for corporate hedging;
- explain the various steps in the financial risk management process;
- understand basic derivatives and their uses.

Theory Highlights from CIMA Official Study System

11.1   The focus of this course is on risk management in the organisation. The following four chapters deal with the role of financial instruments as a measure of risk management. The participants should note that financial market instruments can be approached in three ways namely:

11.1.1   From a risk management or hedging perspective

11.1.2   From an arbitrager perspective (the process of buying and selling a financial instrument simultaneously in two markets)

11.1.3   Speculation.

11.2   The key learning over these four chapters will be to develop an understanding of the mechanisms involved in interest rate and currency derivatives and to distinguish between activities involving risk-averse market instrument management or hedging techniques and the opposite speculative and risk-taking behaviour. In order for the participant to have a good understanding, it will be necessary to practice simulation examples.

11.3   Financial risk management processes involve identifying the risk exposure, quantifying the exposure using either regression analysis, simulation or value-at-risk techniques.

11.4   *Regression method*. Easy to implement, familiar and easy to understand but based on historical data and not necessarily a predictor of future events. This method regresses changes in cash flow against various factors such as changes in interest rates, exchange rates or major commodities such as oil.

11.5 *Simulation method*. Complex and difficult to implement, conceptually complex and thus difficult to explain to non-specialists but is dynamic and can be adapted to different assumptions and circumstances. Unlike the regression method which is based on historic data, simulation analysis is used to evaluate the sensitivity of likely future cash flows to simulated values of various risk factors based on probability distributions of those risk factors. This produces a range of possible cash flows. The greater the standard deviation from the mean, the greater the risk that is associated with the cash flows.

11.6 *Value-at-risk method*. Can be complex with difficult statistical assumptions to implement; it easier to understand and communicate to non-specialists and the outcome is dependent upon underlying assumptions. VaR measures the maximum loss possible due to normal market movements in a given period with a stated probability. Under normal market conditions, losses greater than the value at risk rarely occur. VaR is used widely for measuring exposure to financial price risks.

11.7 The Treasury function is concerned with the relationship between an organization and its financial stakeholders (shareholders, lenders and taxation authorities).

11.8 Treasury activities may be accounted for either as a cost centre or profit centre. Where Treasury acts as a profit centre, business units are charged a market rate for services provided, and the Treasurer is concerned with operating efficiently and making a profit. However, making a profit is a motivation to speculate and arguments can occur over the method of charging between Treasury and business units.

11.9 Companies are exposed to firm-specific risks relating to their own operations and market-wide risks affecting the economic environment of all companies.

11.10 A hedge is a transaction to reduce or eliminate an exposure to risk. Hedging reduces the likelihood and impact of bankruptcy, reduces taxes, reduces the volatility of cash flows and reduces the risk faced by managers.

11.11 A derivative is a financial instrument whose value depends on the price of an underlying. The underlying may be a commodity e.g. oil, gold, shares, interest rates, currencies, etc. Forward contracts, futures, options and swaps are all derivatives that can be used to manage risk. They may be exchange-traded or over-the-counter (OTC) between buyers and sellers.

Theory Revision Questions

The questions in this section are intended to assist you with learning the relevant concepts relating to risk management deploying derivatives. It is important to memorise and learn these concepts and tools for later recall in the examination. After studying this section, you should attempt the questions in Sections 2 and 3. Questions in Sections 2 and 3 enable you to apply these concepts and tools in composite business problem scenarios. The examination is designed around composite scenario problem solving type questions and Sections 2 and 3 have informed mainly on past exam papers as examples for you to prepare appropriately.

11.1 Describe the four main functions of the treasury.

11.2 Describe the key focus for each of the strategic, tactical and operational levels of treasury management.

11.3 What are the benefits of hedging financial risks?

11.4 When could hedging be considered counterproductive?

11.5 Blok-Foster Plc exports blue widgets from England to South Africa. Based upon prominent economists' predictions of economic growth, interest rates and currency movements, B-F Plc estimate that the profit equivalent in GBP from the South African market will range between a high of £25 m, £20 m and a low of £15 m with probabilities of 0.25, 0 and 4, 0.35 respectively.

Calculate the expected value and standard deviation of the profits from the South African market.

11.6 Differentiate between forward contracts and futures contracts.

11.7 For what reason would a major motor manufacturer and a steel mill enter into a forward contract?

11.8 Briefly explain the mechanism of a swap and an option and describe their benefit to the contracting parties.

11.9 What is the difference between hedging and speculative trading in financial instruments?

11.10 Explain how arbitrage trading is conducted.

11.11 Suppose Intertrade Plc receives quotes of US$0.009369–71 for the Yen and US$0.0365–6 for the Taiwan dollar (NT$).

(a) How many US$ will Intertrade receive from the sale of ¥60 million?
(b) What is the US$ cost to Intertrade of buying ¥1 billion?
(c) How many NT$ will Intertrade receive for US$500,000?
(d) How many yen will Intertrade receive for NT$200 million?
(e) What is the US$ cost to Intertrade of buying NT$80 million?

11.12 Suppose the Euro is quoted at 0.6064–80 in London and the Pound Sterling is quoted at 1.6244–59 in Frankfurt.

(a) Is there a profitable arbitrage situation?
(b) Compute the percentage bid-ask spreads on the Pound Sterling and Euro.

11.13 On April 1, the spot price of the British pound was $1.86 and the price of the June futures contract was $1.85. During April the pound appreciated, so that by May 1 it was selling for $1.91.

What do you think happened to the price of the June pound futures contract during April? Explain.

11.14 Suppose the Fluor Group wants to hedge a bid on a Polish construction project. But because the Euro exposure is contingent on acceptance of its bid, Fluor decides to buy a put option for the €15 billion bid amount rather than sell it forward. In order to reduce its hedging costs, however, Fluor simultaneously sells a call option for €15 billion with the same strike price. Fluor reasons that it wants to protect its downside risk on the contract and is willing to sacrifice the upside potential in order to collect the call premium.

Comment on Fluor's hedging strategy.

11.15 Suppose that Macrosoft must pay its French supplier €20 million in 90 days.

(a) Explain how Macrosoft can use currency futures to hedge its exchange risk.
(b) How many futures contracts will Macrosoft need to fully protect itself?
(c) Explain how Macrosoft can use currency options to hedge its exchange risk.
(d) How many options contracts will Macrosoft need to fully protect itself?
(e) Discuss the advantages and disadvantages of using currency futures versus currency options to hedge Macrosoft's exchange risk.

Theory Revision Solutions

11.1 The main functions of the treasury include:

- Banking
- Liquidity management
- Funding management
- Currency management.

11.2 Treasury activities involved at each of the three levels include:

1 *Strategic*: Long-term capital structure of the organisation including cost of capital considerations, balancing equity, debentures, loan capital and investment.
2 *Tactical*: Includes the management of investments and liquidity and involves decisions on hedging of currency and/or interest rate risk.
3 *Operational*: Daily cash banking and surplus cash placement with banks.

11.3 Financial risk hedging includes the following potential benefits:

- Reduces the probability and cost of financial distress
- Has the potential to reduce taxes
- Reduces volatility of cash flows and can increase the value of the company
- Reduce its contracting costs because it reduces the risks faced by managers.

11.4 In certain instances, hedging could be considered counterproductive where:

- Shareholders hold diversified portfolios, hedging could harm rather than enhance shareholders returns.
- Transaction costs, brokerage fees and commissions consume all possible benefits.
- Hesitancy by senior managers due to lack of expertise.
- Complexities associated with tax avoidance and disclosure requirements outweigh the benefits.

11.5 The expected income from the South African market is calculated as follows:

$$E(X) = \sum P_i X_i$$

$$E(X) = (25 \times 0.25) + (20 \times 0.4) + (15 \times 0.35)$$

$$= \pounds19.5M$$

$$
\begin{aligned}
\sigma \quad &= \sqrt{\sum P_i [X_i - E(X)]^2} \\
&= \sqrt{0.25(25 - 19.5)^2 + 0.4(20 - 19.5)^2 + 0.35(15 - 19.5)^2} \\
&= \sqrt{7.5625 + 0.1 + 7.0875} \\
&= \sqrt{14.75} \\
&= \pounds3.84M
\end{aligned}
$$

Profits from the South African market are expected to be £19.5M with a standard deviation of £3.84M.

11.6 Forward contracts are legally binding agreements between two parties to buy or sell an asset at a given time in the future for a given price agreed today. These contracts are generally concluded between the two parties with, possibly a trader intermediary facilitating the process.

Futures contracts oblige the buyer (or seller) to purchase (or sell) the quantity specified in the contract at a predetermined price at the expiration of the contract. Futures contracts usually trade on organised exchanges while forward contracts are OTC contracts.

11.7 The motor manufacturer may wish to fix the price of steel in order to better predict the cost of producing motor vehicles for a specific market. The benefit the motor manufacturer will enjoy will be the knowledge today of the price of steel and for production to be executed in the future.

From the steel mill's point of view, they will know the price and hence their revenue stream that will flow in the future as a result of the fixed price computed with the motor manufacturer. The steel mill will enjoy the benefit of knowing what their future revenue stream will look like today.

Both the steel mill and the motor manufacturer will have negated the risk or foregone the benefit of the commodity steel price at that future date. The benefit to both parties is the knowledge today of the future cost/price they will pay/receive for that volume of the commodity (steel). This facilitates planning and removes uncertainty.

11.8 A swap is a contract between two parties requiring of both parties to deliver, at specified intervals, payments based upon differing rates for a common underlying notional principal. Both parties gain from the swap by participating in the differential between the underlying interest or exchange rates to which the parties are exposed/contracted. The intermediary (bank or brokerage) normally arranges the swap for portion of the shared differential.

An option is a contract that gives the holder the right, but not the obligation, to purchase or sell an underlying commodity on a predetermined future date in exchange for a premium paid today. This enables the purchaser to either cap the cost of a commodity or receive a minimum price, depending upon whether a call or put option is purchased.

11.9 A party, trading for the purposes of hedging, enters the market with a pre-existing exposure to an interest rate or exchange rate. All international business transactions will, in the event of change in market prices/rates, result in a loss to the organisation. Under these conditions, the party enters the marketplace and takes a position with a financial instrument to soften the impact of potential changes, thus reducing the impact of the loss.

A speculator, on the other hand, is a party that enters the marketplace for financial instruments-based upon a notion or hunch that a particular commodity, interest or exchange rate will-move in a particular direction. This party does not necessarily have a pre-existing exposure and will, therefore, be exposed to the full effect of the rate or price of the underlying principal.

11.10 Arbitrage is the process of trading in a common financial instrument in two markets for a common underlying commodity or principal. The arbitrageur thus simultaneously purchases a commodity or principal in one market and sells it in another at the same time.

Arbitrageurs thus have access and knowledge to multiple markets and are able to exploit price differences at a given time. Arbitrage is risk neutral because the benefit to the arbitrageur accrues without time or further trading risk.

11.11

Part	Working	Answer	Units
(a)	60,000,000 × 0.009369 =	562,140	US$
(b)	1,000,000,000 × 0.009371 =	9,371,000	US$
(c)	500,000/0.0366 =	13,661,202	NT$
(d)	(200,000,000 × 0.009369)/0.0366 =	51,196,721	NT$
(e)	80,000,000 × 0.0366 =	2,928,000	US$

11.12

Part	Working	Answer	Units
(a)			
Buy £ in Frankfurt	€1,000,000/1.6259	615,043.98	Pounds
Sell £ in London	£615,043.98/0.608	1,011,585.49	Euro
Buy € in London	€1,000,000/0.608 =	1,644,736.84	
Sell € in Frankfurt	€1,644,736.84/1.628 =	1,010,280.62	
(b)			
London	(0.608 − 0.6064)/0.608 × 100 =	0.2632	% (1)
Frankfurt	(1.6259 − 1.6244)/1.6259 × 100 =	0.0923	% (2)
Difference	(1) − (2) =	0.1709	%

11.13

Description	Working	Amounts	Units
01/04/2006 Spot	Given	1.86	(1)
01/05/2006 Spot	Given	1.91	(2)
% Change	(1) − (2) =	0.026882	
01/04/2006 Future	Given	1.85	$
01/05/2006 Future	Estimated change	1.899731	$

Given that the Pound Sterling has appreciated against the US$, we would expect the future for the currency to appreciate in sympathy at approximately the same rate as the appreciation for the spot rate.

 It is important to note that the futures pricing will be dependent upon expectation in the market and may appreciate even more than the spot rate if the exchange rate is expected to appreciate further. The appreciation of the pound may, however, be seen as a short-term reaction to a transient event and is expected to return to a weaker position later. In that case, it is more likely that a lower appreciation of the future can be expected.

11.14   The selection of a PUT option over a future or forward contract places Fluor in a position to decide at a later date to either execute the option or not dependent upon the outcome of the contract and the exchange rate circumstances at the time. If the contract is not concluded and there is no material change in the exchange rate, the PUT option is simply abandoned. If, however, the exchange rate had changed materially and the contract was concluded, Fluor would have secured the returns based on the rates providing at the time of the bid.

By simultaneously negotiating a CALL option, Fluor would be in a position to settle the CALL with the proceeds of the PUT and receive the premium that would all set the premium paid for the PUT. This mechanism works well, provided the strike price for both the PUT and CALL is the same. If the strike prices for both are not identical, the gap would result in a potential loss.

If the contract is in fact concluded, then the currency would be required for conversion into US$ and Fluor would be left with the CALL exposure.

11.15

(a) Macrosoft would negotiate 160 currency futures. The limitation will be the maturity date which may not coincide exactly what the 90-day payment. Macrosoft may have to negotiate a revised payment date or suffer the exposure between the futures maturity date and the payment date with the supplier. A complication of this method is that daily settlement is required resulting in a substantial administrative and cash flow commitment.

(b) 20,000,000/125,000 = 160 futures contracts

(c) Macrosoft could negotiate a PUT option that will protect the currency conversion rate. Depending upon the style of option purchased, the contract size will vary. Assuming that the option is traded on the Philadelphia stock exchange, the value per contract would be €62,500. If the option is an American-style option, the option can be exercised at any time before or on the expiring date. If the option is a European-style option then it can only be exercised on the maturity date. While options are more expensive than futures or forwards they do leave the purchaser with the option to exercise their right or not. This enables the purchaser to take advantage of any profits if the exchange rate should do in their favour.

(d) 20,000,000/62,500 = 320 options contracts

(e) Currency futures are cheaper than currency options but that is where the advantages end.

The following are the disadvantages of using futures:

- Potential gaps between the maturity date of the futures and the payment date of the debt to the supplier;
- The futures impose an obligation on the purchaser to execute whereas the option provides the purchaser with the right but not the obligation to execute. This flexibility comes at a cost which has to be weighed against the benefits of retaining the right not to execute;
- Futures contracts require daily matching-to-market which involves both administrative and cash flow obligations on a daily basis.

Interest Rate Management

Interest Rate Management

12

LEARNING OUTCOMES

After completing this chapter in the CIMA *Learning System* you should be able to

- interpret the risks facing an organisation that arise from movements in interest rates;
- identify and evaluate appropriate methods for managing interest rate risk;
- demonstrate how and when to convert fixed rate interest to floating rate interest;
- illustrate the effect of interest rate risk management techniques such as swaps, forward rate agreements, futures, options and swaptions.

Theory Highlights from CIMA Official Study System

12.1 This chapter focuses on the organisation's exposure to interest rate risk. Every organisation is exposed to capital cost dependent upon their equity structure and sources and availability of debt in the markets in which they raise capital.

12.2 In this highly competitive world, businesses cannot allow cash reserves to lie idle. Treasury will have the task of maximising the earnings from investments while critically balancing operational and project cash requirements.

12.3 To a large extent, interest rate risk arises out of timing differences between cash commitments and cash receipts. In order to ensure adequate capital availability, organisations have to maintain reserves on the one hand and negotiate borrowings on the other.

12.4 Our task is to identify instances and periods of exposure to interest rate risk and, being risk averse and therefore not speculative in terms of interest rate, would seek to minimise those risks.

12.5 The impact of interest rates on the business therefore depends upon the choice or availability of funding. The exposures arise due to:

    12.5.1 The mix between capital and debt

    12.5.2 The mix between fixed and floating rate debt

    12.5.3 The mix between short-term and long-term debt.

12.6   The instruments are available to us for this purpose includes:

    12.6.1   Internal hedging techniques which comprise:

        12.6.1.1   *Smoothing*: Fixed and variable interest rates debt is negotiated or deployed in equal amounts and thus balancing the exposure which naturally provides a hedge, one against the other.

        12.6.1.2   *Matching*: Funding investments with debt instruments that have a similar interest exposure – e.g.: fixed interest rate income funded by fixed interest rate debt.

        12.6.1.3   *Netting*: Both assets and liability positions are aggregated to determine the net exposure.

    12.6.2   External hedging includes:

        12.6.2.1   Interest rate swaps
        12.6.2.2   Forward rate agreements
        12.6.2.3   Interest rate futures
        12.6.2.4   Interest rate options
        12.6.2.5   Caps, floors and collars
        12.6.2.6   Hybrid techniques such as swaptions.

12.7   The choice of instrument to use is dependent upon availability in the market, cost–benefit considerations, risk appetite and timescale.

12.8   Hedging decisions will depend on the circumstances of each company, including:

- the company's objectives
- its risk profile and risk appetite
- the resources available for risk management
- the availability of appropriate hedging products
- the amount of exposure compared to the company's size
- the Treasurer's view as to whether rates will move in the company's favour
- the cost of hedging relative to the company's exposure.

Theory Revision Questions

The questions in this section are intended to assist you with learning the relevant concepts relating to interest rate management. It is important to memorise and learn these concepts and tools for later recall in the examination. After studying this section, you should attempt the questions in Sections 2 and 3. Questions in Sections 2 and 3 enable you to apply these concepts and tools in composite business problem scenarios. The examination is designed around composite scenario problem solving type questions and Sections 2 and 3 have informed mainly on past exam papers as examples for you to prepare appropriately.

12.1   What is the difference between credit and market risk?

12.2   What is meant by matching in the hedging context?

12.3   Companies X and Y wish to negotiate a swap based on a notional £50 million, 5-year loan. Their credit profiles enable them to offers from lenders as follows:

	Fixed Rate	Floating Rate
Company X:	5.5%	LIBOR + 0.1%
Company Y:	6.5%	LIBOR + 0.4%

Company X requires a floating rate loan and company Y requires a fixed rate loan. Design a swap that will net the bank, acting as intermediary, 0.1% per annum and that will appear equally attractive to both companies.

12.4   Forward rate agreements applied

JD & Co Plc has a covenant with its lenders of EBITDA/interest <4 times cover. The total outstanding loan balance is £230 million and is all variable interest bearing. Market expectation is that interest rates are set to rise in the UK due to inflationary pressures from 6% to 7% p.a. GDP growth is expected to fall and market conditions are likely to harden. Indications from marketing are that sales are expected to fall sharply and EBITDA returns for this financial year will drop to £60 million. Planning for the next 3-years has also revealed that market conditions were expected to remain suppressed or-recover to current conditions if the oil price dropped.

Janet Henry, the CFO, has investigated the market and established that Euros denominated loans can be secured at 6.2% subject to identical conditions applicable to existing loans and attracts a 1% raising fee. A £ denominated FRA is available at 6.5%. Fixed interest rate loans in £ are available at 7%.

Janet has approached you for advice. What would you recommend her to do?

12.5   Interest-futures applied

This question extends the discussion in question 4.

Your investigations suggest that interest futures are available at a price of 93.7. The IRF covers the period to 1 month past the financial year end.

The market for interest rate options suggest a strike price of 6.35% at the identical close-out date as the IRF. The premium is £2000.

How would this additional information affect your recommendation to Janet?

12.6   Interest rate options applied – cap

This question extends the discussion in questions 4 and 5.

Janet was about to implement your advice (question 5 continued) when she mentioned that the loan was, in fact, for a 5-year period of which 4 years would be remaining at the financial year end.

Further investigation, in the light of this additional information revealed that a 4-year 6.5% cap on a £230 million loan limit will attract a premium of £2300 and if the cap is combined with a floor of 6.2%, the premium will be £1100.

How does this new knowledge affect your recommendation?

Theory Revision Solutions

12.1 Credit risk is the risk that party A assumes when contracting with party B that relates to party B failing to meet its obligations. Credit risk is thus transaction-specific and relates to the contracting parties only.

Market risk is risk that all parties in a particular market will be exposed to. Market risk is therefore, not party-specific that translates to external changes that have an impact on the contracting parties.

 Market risk could, however, be a forerunner/indicator of credit risk in the sense that, if party B defaulted on the contract (credit risk) as a result of a steep rise interest rates (market risk) then credit risk considerations should be evaluated in terms of market risk.

12.2 Matching, in the hedging sense, is an internal hedging technique deployed where the organisation is in a position to negotiate funding arrangements that match their market conditions. For example, should an organisation have fixed price contracts, funding should be arranged on a fixed rate basis to avoid interest rate risk.

12.3 The structure of an interest rate swap, leaving both parties equally satisfied and arranging bank loan with 0.1% commission, could be effected as follows:

	Company X	Company Y	Quality Spread
Fixed Rate:	5.5%	6.5%	1.0
Floating Rate:	LIBOR + 0.1	LIBOR + 0.4	0.3
Differential			0.7

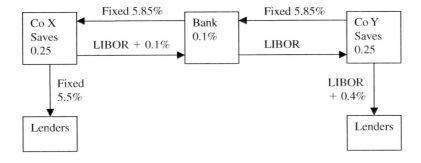

Company X: Acquires variable rate and saves 0.25%;
Company Y: Acquires fixed rate and saves 0.25%
Bank: Assumes credit risk and receives 0.1% commission

12.4 In preparation for my advice to you Janet, I have presented the following analysis:

The covenant with the lenders will require that you keep interest repayments below £15 M (£60 M/4) based upon projected EBITDA.

Variable Loan (assume rise to 7%) (£230 M × 7%)	£16.10 M p.a.
Euro Loan (£230 M in Euro equivalent × 6.2%)	£14.26 M p.a.
Hedged (£16.10 M − (£230 M × (7% − FRA £230 × 6.5%)))	£14.95 M p.a.

The most favourable option would be to accept the Euro-based loan provided that you are prepared to accept the related currency risk.

Fixed rates fall outside of the covenant range and are not advisable.

The FRA hedged option results in a cost adjustment of £0.69 M and offers the most cost-effective option under conditions of fully hedged market risk.

My recommendation is to accept the FRA.

12.5   Given the additional information, I have considered your position and recommend that you consider another solution.

Additional findings:

Option: Variable Loan (assume 7%) (£230M × 7%)	£16.10M p.a
Less: Option pay-out (7 − 6.35%)	£1.4605M p.a.
Add: Fee	£0.001M p.a.
Cost	£14.6405M p.a.

The option should be selected when there is fair certainty that the interest 'rate will exceed 6.36%.

This option provided more freedom and leaves you free to pay lower interest should the rate not rise as high as expected and provides cover for the covenant limit.

12.6   Covering the covenant limit at year end is part of the solution required. The loan is for 4 future years and therefore, if market conditions do not improve, future covenant exposure is likely.

Covering the full loan period is required.

The negotiation of a cap would result in the following:

Cap (£230 M × 6.5%)	14.95 M
Fee	0.02 M
Cost	14.97 M

The cap satisfies the covenant, should interest rates rise above 6.5%.

The floor will result in a saving of £1000 but could preclude the company from paying interest at 6%, should the conditions return to current status. Assuming 6% in any future year, the company will lose £3600 p.a.

The better choice is a cap without a floor which provides flexibility to follow the lower market and cover the covenant in all future years.

Foreign Exchange: Relationships and Risks

Foreign Exchange: Relationships and Risks

13

Theory Highlights from CIMA Official Study System

13.1   In a globalising world, foreign exchange risk has become a prominent feature of business life. The majority of countries now operated floating exchange rates with the result that international trade is subject to exchange rate uncertainty and risk.

13.2   The hedging instruments available for exchange rate management are similar to interest rate instruments. The complexity lies in establishing expected exchange rate movements based on economic dynamics in the marketplace.

13.3   Theoretical Forex relationships include speculation, balance of payments, government policy, and interest rate differentials and inflation rate differentials. Numerous modelling tools are available and we concern ourselves with the following:

       13.3.1   Interest rate parity model
       13.3.2   Purchasing power parity model
       13.3.3   The Fisher effect
       13.3.4   Expectation theory.

13.4   Deriving its rationale from monetary economic mechanisms, exchange rates correlate with money market rates. International investment money follows markets where high interest rates prevail. Because arbitrage will move markets closer and close opportunity gaps, we can assume a reasonably efficient market. The relationship between the interest rates and the spot and forward exchange rates enables us to calculate the expected exchange rate one period ahead.

13.5   The purchasing power model is premised upon the assumption that, where a country has a higher rate of inflation than its trading partners, that country's exchange rate will fall to realign the purchasing power parity.

13.6   The Fisher effect explains the exchange rates moving in reverse relationship with interest rate movement linked to inflation rate rise/fall.

13.7   Interest rate parity and purchasing power parity assume active arbitrage with a blind spot when investors agree that one currency is riskier than others.

13.8   The risk profile faced, when international trade and investment are undertaken, extends to exchange rate transaction and translation risks, political and economic risk.

13.9   Transaction risk impacts on the organisation's cash flow as well as its performance as measured from its home currency.

13.10   Translation risk relates to the impact on the valuation of foreign assets and liabilities when valued in the reporting currency. The impact is mainly on the funding and valuation issues and can have the effect of influencing credit ratings and borrowing power.

13.11   Political risk has few objective determinants and can often be exaggerated by rumour and contagion rather than being based upon events on the ground. The actions of governments do have substantial shift effect when there is a risk of expropriation, discrimination or the imposition of specific rules regarding ownership, labour or materials.

13.12   The existence of risk deters most and that creates opportunity for others to exploit gaps and structures to their advantage. Knowledge becomes the critical success factor.

Theory Revision Questions

The questions in this section are intended to assist you with learning the relevant concepts relating to relationships and risks of foreign exchange. It is important to memorise and learn these concepts and tools for later recall in the examination. After studying this section, you should attempt the questions in Sections 2 and 3. Questions in Sections 2 and 3 enable you to apply these concepts and tools in composite business problem scenarios. The examination is designed around composite scenario problem solving type questions and Sections 2 and 3 have informed mainly on past exam papers as examples for you to prepare appropriately.

13.1 Distinguish between spot and forward rates.

13.2 What is the difference between interest rate parity and purchasing power parity?

13.3 What does the Fisher effect endeavour to explain?

13.4 What is the effect of exchange rate movements on transactional risk?

13.5 What is the effect of exchange rate movements on translational risk?

13.6 Explain the difference between direct and indirect quote in buying and selling other currencies.

13.7 The exchange rate for the $US against the £stg is $1.884/£ and for the Euro against £stg is €1.603/£. What is the cross-rate of dollars per euro?

13.8 Explain the factors that influence a currency's exchange rate.

13.9 Explain the difference between transaction, economic, translation and political risks.

✓ Theory Revision Solutions

13.1 The spot rate is the exchange rate for a transaction that is due for immediate delivery, while the forward rate applies to a transaction to be conducted sometime in the future.

13.2 Where a country has interest rates higher than those applicable in other countries, they will attract foreign investment which, in turn, will result in a rise in that country's currency exchange rate.

The purchasing power parity model is premised upon currencies being dependent upon/moving in response to differential inflation rates. According to this model, country's experiencing a higher inflation rate than others will be subject to currency devaluation to restore purchasing power equilibrium.

Both the interest rate parity model and the purchasing power parity model rely upon a high level of arbitrage activity to bring about quick adjustments to market rates resulting in an efficient market. Both of these models negate the effects/potential for political or country risks.

13.3 The Fisher effect derives a monetary interest rate from the product of real interest and the country's inflation rate. This mechanism is premised upon monetary economic policy where countries endeavour to limit inflationary pressures through interest rate mechanisms. Higher interest rates have the effect of cooling economic growth and, thereby containing inflation. In the absence of political or country risk considerations, the anticipated effect of an increase in inflation will result in increased interest rates. Increased interest rates will attract foreign investors that, in turn, will purchase the currency driving its rate up.

13.4 The effect of exchange rate movements on transaction risk is to reduce/increase earnings in the home country as a result of the change in exchange rate of a foreign country in which the organisation trades. Cash flow and profitability are both affected.

13.5 Translation risk is the effect of disclosing the value of foreign held assets in home currency terms. A decline in exchange rates will diminish the asset value reported by the organisation with corresponding negative borrowing power as a result of a weekend balance sheet.

13.6 Exchange rates show the price of a currency relative to the price of another currency. A direct quote is the number of domestic currency units needed to buy one unit of a foreign currency. An indirect quote is the number of foreign currency units needed to buy one unit of the domestic currency.

13.7 $\dfrac{\$ \text{ per } £}{€ \text{ per } £}$

$= \dfrac{1.884}{1.603}$

$= 1.1753$ dollars per euro

13.8 The factors that influence a currency's exchange rate include speculation, where a speculator aims to make a profit from the future movement of a currency rather than due to any need for that currency. A country's balance of payments position will also affect the demand and/or supply of that currency. Government policy any influence the value of their currency through devaluations, revaluations or buying or selling on foreign exchange markets. Interest rate differentials create a demand for a currency where investors will buy a currency to earn higher interest rates. Differences in inflation rates between countries, the value of a currency may be falling in real terms compared with others.

13.9   Transaction risk results from the change in exchange rates in relation to a company's contractual obligations (those that have been entered but not yet settled) for cash flows and arises from selling or buying goods in other countries, from borrowing or lending money in other currencies, or from foreign currency denominated derivatives. Economic risk relates to exchange rate fluctuations on future cash flows before a transaction takes place. Even domestically operating companies face economic risk from foreign competitors acting in local markets. Translation risk does not affect cash flow but affects the balance sheet valuation of assets and liabilities held in foreign currencies where exchange rates change relative to the home currency. Political risk results from political acts by foreign governments.

14

Foreign Exchange Risk Management

Foreign Exchange Risk Management 14

LEARNING OUTCOMES

After completing this chapter in CIMA *Learning System* you should be able to

- recommend foreign exchange risk management strategies;
- identify the different types of internal hedging techniques;
- calculate the optimum hedging technique, giving consideration to the forward market, the money market, futures and options;
- illustrate the use of currency swaps.

Theory Highlights from CIMA Official Study System

14.1 Foreign exchange risk, as with interest rate risk, can be internally and externally managed.

14.2 Internal management techniques include home currency invoicing, bilateral and multilateral netting, leading and lagging techniques, matching and restructuring.

14.3 External hedging techniques include forward contracts, futures, options and swaps.

14.4 The theory relating to these techniques was dealt with in Chapters 11,12 and 13 and will, therefore, not be repeated here.

14.5 The international accounting standards and the international financial reporting standards have brought about substantial additional disclosure requirements. IAS21 has been adapted, requiring transactions to be recognised at the exchange rate on the date of the original transaction, non-cash assets to be reported at the date of acquisition or revaluation and cash or near-cash instruments to be translated at the reporting date. IFRS3 requires that intangible assets be disclosed at transaction value and be subjected to impairment adjustments annually.

14.6 The implications of these disclosure requirements for the organisation are:

14.6.1 Substantially increased costs of record-keeping.

14.6.2 Disclosure parameters that could expose strategic detail to competitors.

14.6.3 Management choices that try to avoid the complexity and, in so doing, unwittingly leave the organisation open to risk.

14.6.4 The subjectivity of country and political risk leaves the organisation vulnerable and, therefore careful and comprehensive hedging of currency risk is important.

14.7 Futures in foreign exchange rates are contracts to buy or sell an amount of foreign currency at a future date and are traded on futures exchanges. An option in foreign exchange rates gives the client the right – but not the obligation – to buy (a call option) or sell (a put option) a specific amount of foreign currency at a specific price on a specific date.

14.8 Where a company has a foreign currency risk, it may hedge against the currency risk by using forward markets or money markets. The method selected will be the one that leads to the smallest payment or the highest receipt in the home currency.

14.9 A currency swap is the regular exchange of interest or cash flows in one currency for that of another. There is an exchange of principal at the beginning and end of the swap contract which are useful for medium-to long-term hedging (over one year).

Theory Revision Questions

The questions in this section are intended to assist you with learning the relevant concepts relating to foreign exchange risk management. It is important to memorise and learn these concepts and tools for later recall in the examination. After studying this section, you should attempt the questions in Sections 2 and 3. Questions in Sections 2 and 3 enable you to apply these concepts and tools in composite business problem scenarios. The examination is designed around composite scenario problem solving type questions and Sections 2 and 3 have informed mainly on past exam papers as examples for you to prepare appropriately.

14.1 Explain the internal hedging technique: bilateral netting.

14.2 How does an organisation deploy a lead or lag measure to hedge a currency exposure?

14.3 What steps can an organisation take to restructure so as to reduce their long-term exposure to exchange rate fluctuations?

14.4 What problems could an organisation encounter with currency forward contracts?

14.5 What is meant by the term 'in the money' and how does that affect the premium of an option?

14.6 Multi-National Traders Plc comprises a group of companies controlled from the UK. The company has branches in China, Germany and Botswana.

The inter-company indebtedness as at 30th June 2006 was as follows:

- The Chinese subsidiary is owed RMB955,342,000 by the Botswanan subsidiary and owes the German subsidiary €1,203,500;
- The German subsidiary owes the Botswanan subsidiary €1,254,665 and is owed RMB722,765,320 by the Chinese subsidiary.
- The Chinese subsidiary owes the Botswanan subsidiary P347,897,000.

The central treasury department has a policy of netting-off inter-company balances as far as possible and issued instructions for settlement of the net balances between the subsidiaries. For the purposes of netting, the central treasury set the following exchange rates:

- Botswanan Pula   £1 = P5.22
- Euro   £1 = €1.78
- Chinese Renminbi   £1 = RMB27.40

(a)   Calculate the debt payments by each subsidiary.
(b)   What obstacles could the central treasury department experience with multilateral netting?

14.7 Poinou Plc manufactures and distributes a range of household linen in 10 countries. The fabric is produced in Thailand and stitched in Korea then exported to subsidiary branches across Europe, UK and USA.

Owing to global economic conditions, the company anticipates that the Korean Won (KRW) will once again depreciate substantially in two months' time.

The group CEO has requested that you take measures to limit any losses and capitalize on the upside, as far as possible, from the declining KRW.

The subsidiary companies have provided you with payments due in 30 days as follows:

Euro based	€221,434,589 owed to the Korean subsidiary by European subsidiaries
GB Pound	£3,467,312 owed to the Korean subsidiary by UK subsidiaries
US Dollar	$16,962,715 owed to the Korean subsidiary by US subsidiaries
Korean Won	₩650,455,630 owed by the Korean subsidiary to the Thai manufacturing subsidiary.

Recommend an efficient inter-subsidiary settlement strategy.

14.8   How is the strategy approach in 14.7 affected if the Korean government implemented exchange control?

14.9   Assume that key indicators point to a devaluation of the US dollar in relation to other currencies instead of the Korean Won as stated in 14.7. How would this turn of events influence your inter-subsidiary settlement strategy?

14.10 Suppose that IBM would like to borrow floating-rate yen, whereas African Development Bank (ADB) would like to borrow fixed-rate dollars. IBM can borrow fixed rate dollars at 3.9% or floating rate yen at LIBOR plus 0.25%. ADB can borrow fixed-rate dollars at 4.9% or floating-rate yen at LIBOR plus 0.80%.

(a)   What is the range of possible cost savings that IBM can realize through an interest rate/currency swap with ADB?

(b)   Assume a notional principle is equivalent to $125 million and a current exchange rate of ¥105/$, what do these possible cost savings translate to in yen terms?

Theory Revision Solutions

14.1   Bilateral netting is a technique employed by subsidiaries within an organisation. These subsidiaries net-off their debit and credit positions leaving the residual exposed to currency risk that then has to be hedged externally.

> Multilateral netting applies where an organisation nets off between subsidiaries from a central office.

14.2   Lead and lag techniques involve the organisation in practices where transactions are rescheduled to take advantage of a currency change or anticipated change. A lead measure would be applied where payment is required early for performance to take place later. Lag measures could involve arranging for payment to be delayed to capitalise on anticipated currency strengthening.

14.3   Restructuring an organisation is normally a long-term solution to a problem. Where sustained advantage or disadvantage is perceived in multi-currency markets, the organisation should take measures to capitalise on opportunities and avoid deteriorating conditions. Specific measures include:

- Increasing sales where opportunities abound and reduce sales in deteriorating currency markets;
- Increased dependency upon foreign suppliers where currency deterioration favours cost cutting and vice versa where currency depreciation makes pricing unfavourable;
- Establishing manufacturing facilities in weak currency markets and closing/selling production facilities in markets where currency appreciation reduces competitiveness;
- Incurring new debt facilities denominated in a foreign currency where that currency is weakening; making it cheaper when seen from the home currency perspective and liquidating debt denominated in a foreign currency where it is appreciating.

14.4   Forward exchange contracts are binding. As a result, when conditions change making the contract unfavourable, the organisation is bound by the contract and will incur the negative effects imposed. The rationale for these products is to bring about certainty. The price (opportunity cost) that the organisation pays for certainty is the loss of access to changes in the opposite direction that would otherwise result in a benefit.

Where availability or needs change, the organisation will be required to top-up any shortfall or over-pay where forward cover arrangements exceed the final requirements.

In extreme cases, where the supplier defaults or political circumstances substantially alter trading conditions, the organisation remains obligated to proceed with the contract is respectively.

14.5   The term 'in the money' refers to a condition where the strike price is more favourable to the clients than is currently available. Under these conditions, the premium payable will likely be higher.

14.6

Step 1   *Paying Subsidiaries*

Receiving Subsidiaries	*Botswana*	*Chinese*	*German*
Botswana		P347,897,000	€1,254,665
Chinese	RMB955, 342,000		
German		€1,203,500 RMB722,765,320	

Step 2	*Botswana*	*Chinese*	*German*	*Total Receipts*	*Net Pay/(Rec)*
Botswana		66,646,934.87	704,867.98	67,351,802.84	32,485,306.49
Chinese	34,866,496.35			34,866,496.35	−58,834,858.46
German		676,123.60 26,378,296.35		676,123.60 26,378,296.35	26,349,551.97
Total Payments	34,866,496.35	93,701,354.81	704,867.98	129,272,719.14	–

14.7

Paying Subsidiaries

Receiving Subsidiaries	*European*	*UK*	*USA*	*Korea*
Korea	€221,434 589	£3,467,312	$16,962,715	
Thailand				₩650,455,630

The above table reflects the payments due to the Korean subsidiary and those payments payable by the Koreans subsidiary to the Thai subsidiary.

Numerous alternatives are possible dependent upon the trading circumstances of each subsidiary. Ideally speaking, all payments to the Korean subsidiary should be deferred for as long as possible to maximize the amount of profit possible from the declining Korean won. Payments by the Korean subsidiary to the Thai subsidiary would be accelerated and paid immediately.

The above approach assumes that the Korean subsidiary has the available capital reserves to pay its debts while deferring its receipts. In the event that the Korean subsidiary requires payment before it can execute payment to the Thai subsidiary, the approach would be to pay from that currency that reflects the least appreciation against the Korean won as compared with other currencies owed. Only sufficient funds would be paid to the Korean subsidiary to cover its required cash flow balance. The remaining funds owing would be deferred for as long as possible.

 Additional considerations would include the terms and conditions of the exchange controls possibly and posed by the Korean authorities, the interest rates applicable in each of the countries and taxation. If offsets are possible, the paying subsidiaries could settle the Thai expenses directly on behalf of the Korean subsidiary.

14.8 In the event that the Korean authorities implemented exchange control, payments to the Thai subsidiary may be delayed and restrictions upon the deferment of receipts may be imposed. Under these conditions, careful consideration would have to be given to redirecting payments directly to the Thai subsidiary and only then settling the Korean debt remaining.

 Experience has shown that, when countries experience currency problems, trading conditions deteriorate and the local subsidiaries are placed under pressure. In a globalizing world, it is often advisable to establish more than one subsidiary to carry out production activities in order to build in redundancy into the system to reduce the negative impact of adverse sovereign decisions.

14.9   If the US$ started to decline against the other traded currencies, payments from the US to Korea would be accelerated and, payments in respect of future shipments may also be accelerated to avoid the impact on the pricing in the American market. Alternative strategies could include the nuclear issue nation of forward contracts, futures or options.

14.10

(a)

	Fixed Rate	Floating Rate
IBM	3.9	LIBOR + 0.25
ADB	4.9	LIBOR + 0.80
Difference	1	0.55
Available for Swap		0.45

The organizations are in a position to exploit the 45 basis points difference between their borrowing rates. They are able to effect a swap and share the 45 basis points between them.

 In this example, the assumption is made that IBM seeks yen exposure and ADB seeks US$ exposure. In other words, these parties wish to gain access to a currency and, in the process, are able to exploit the differential in their borrowing capacity. Also, they must want exposure to differing loan bases of fixed and variable interest.

(b)

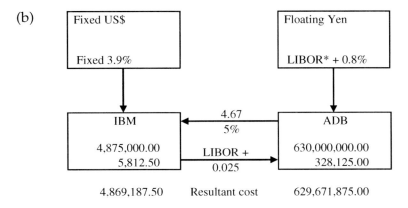

* LIBOR is assumed to be 4% and a single annual period is applied.

At the expiry of twelve months (one year), the parties will settle their respective interest payments to each other at the ruling exchange rate at that date but based upon the original amount swapped. IBM saves \$5,812.50 and ADB saves ¥328,125.00 and each gains the exposure to the borrowing basis and currency they desire. IBM will gain the benefit of the variable-rate loan and carry the risk of any loss. They will then pay their debt in yen with no exposure to exchange rate movements. Similarly, ADB will gain the benefit of fixed-rate US\$ and pay bills in US\$ free of the exchange rate risk.

Section 2
Topic – Oriented Exam
Questions and Answers
with Approach Suggestions

Topic – Oriented Exam Questions and Answers with Approach Suggestions

Section 2

This section contains questions that are extracted from or typical of Part B of the exam paper. Typically, these questions carry 25 marks. A choice of two out of four questions is available. However, each question typically covers more than one aspect of the course content. Mostly, the questions test the student's ability to demonstrate their ability to relate the content to practical business situations and to synthesise the content of the module into solutions to business challenges.

Answer Structuring Tool

To help you develop answers to the questions, I have suggested a process which I have called the R.A.I.D.© method. By following this method, you should be empowered to structure your analysis of the questions and formulate the answers to the expectations of the examiner.

 R.A.I.D.© – The process of answering an application question follows the following steps:

Read the "Required" first before you read the body of the question.

Analyse the question for its <u>subject</u> and <u>objective(s).</u>

Identify tools, techniques and theory that will aid and support your solution.

Draft your answer with marks in mind.

RISK & CONTROLS (a) & AUDIT (b)

May 2008 – Question Two

CSX is a distribution company, which buys and sells small electronic components. The company has sales of $200 million per annum on which it achieves a profit of $12 million.

Central Warehouse Department

The company has a large Central Warehouse Department employing 100 staff over 2 shifts. The warehouse contains 30,000 different components, which are of high value and are readily saleable. Technological change is commonplace and components can become obsolete with little warning. Twice a year, the Purchasing Manager authorises the disposal of obsolete inventory. Inventory control is carried out through a computer system that has been used by the company for the last ten years.

Purchasing and receiving

Inventory is ordered using manual purchase orders based on tender prices. Goods received into the Central Warehouse are recorded on a manual Goods Received Note which is the source document for computer data entry. Data entry is done by clerical staff employed within the Central Warehouse.

Customer orders

Orders from customers are entered into the computer by clerical staff in the Sales Department. The computer checks inventory availability and produces a Picking List which is used by Central Warehouse staff to assemble the order. Frequently, there are differences between the computer inventory record and what is physically in the store. The Picking List (showing the actual quantities ready to be delivered) is used by clerical staff to update the computer records in the Central Warehouse. A combined Delivery Note/Invoice is then printed to accompany the goods.

Accounting

At the end of each financial year, a physical check of inventory is carried out which results in a significant write-off. To allow for these losses, the monthly operating statements to the Board of Directors include a 2% contingency, added to each month's cost of sales.

Internal Audit Department

The company's Internal Audit Department has been asked by the Board to look at the problem of inventory losses. Managers in the Central Warehouse believe that inventory losses are the result of inaccurate data entry, the old and unreliable nature of the computer system and the large number of small inventory items which are easily lost, or which warehouse staff throw away if they are obsolete or damaged.

 It is very important to note that the above statement guides the thinking towards the response expected by the examiner in terms of the content of the "Required" in this question but this may not always be the case. Be sure to read the required before attempting to read the question so as not to form an opinion of the answer YOU are expecting the examiner to ask.

Requirements

(a) Explain the risks faced by CSX in relation to its inventory control system and recommend specific improvements to the system's internal controls.

(15 marks)

(b) Recommend (without being specific to the CSX scenario) the tests or techniques, both manual and computerised, that internal auditors can use in assessing the adequacy of inventory controls.

(10 marks)

(Total for Question Two = 25 marks)

Response Preparation Suggestions May 2008 – Question Two

$\mathcal{R}$ **Question Two required – Part (a)**

(a) Explain the risks faced by CSX in relation to its inventory control system and recommend specific improvements to the system's internal controls.

$\mathcal{A}$

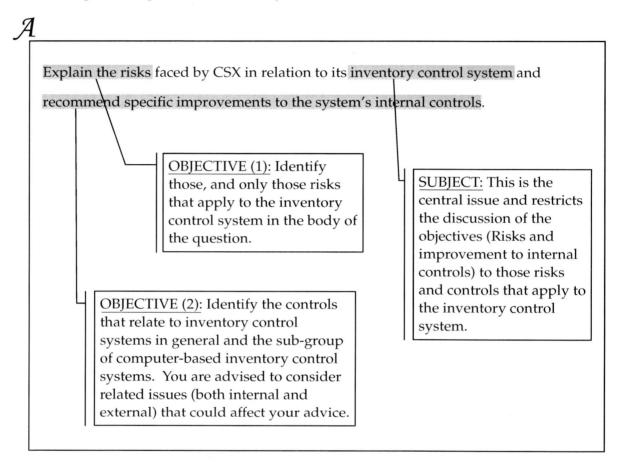

Explain the risks faced by CSX in relation to its inventory control system and recommend specific improvements to the system's internal controls.

OBJECTIVE (1): Identify those, and only those risks that apply to the inventory control system in the body of the question.

OBJECTIVE (2): Identify the controls that relate to inventory control systems in general and the sub-group of computer-based inventory control systems. You are advised to consider related issues (both internal and external) that could affect your advice.

SUBJECT: This is the central issue and restricts the discussion of the objectives (Risks and improvement to internal controls) to those risks and controls that apply to the inventory control system.

I

SUBJECT: Inventory control system: Chapter 8 details the role of IS, IT and IM systems to inform strategic, tactical and operations (in this case: transactional processing and risk management) decisions.

The IM, IT and IS systems could be subjected to Critical Success Factor and Key Performance Indicator (CSF/KPI) analysis to determine the requirements to meet the objectives of reducing the shrinkage through improved controls.

Systems analysis can be deployed to evaluate the features, functions and processes controlling the INPUT-PROCESS-OUTPUT performance of the existing system and then develop the required system to meet the processes, outputs and controls required to manage the risks (to be identified below) and to incorporate the controls necessary to meet the shrinkage reduction objectives in addition to the existing operational requirements the system is already delivering.

Continues . . .

OBJECTIVE 1: Inventory control system risks: Risk types: Business and Operational probably comprising:

> ➤ Errors of commission or omission by employees in processes resulting in:
>   - ○ Stock outages that frustrate customers and loss of business
>   - ○ Over-ordering resulting in unnecessary working capital being tied up
>   - ○ Unnecessary redundancy risk
>   - ○ Over-payments to suppliers
>   - ○ Loss of discounts due to delays in data capture resulting in late payments to suppliers
>   - ○ Inventory item location duplication
>   - ○ Omission of inventory item record altogether
>   - ○ Incorrect item disposal

> ➤ IM, IT & IS systems failure

> ➤ Business interruptions

> ➤ Fraud and theft

OBJECTIVE 2: General system's internal controls:

> ➤ General design requirements for an effective control system – (See Ch 1)
>   - ○ Specifically the Otley & Berry conditions for a controlled process.

> ➤ Inventory controls (See Q6.9 in Ch 6)

> ➤ Auditing

OBJECTIVE 2 (Sub-objective): Computer-based system's internal controls:

> ➤ Security, integrity and contingencies – (See Ch 9)

> ➤ Input, process and output controls.

> ➤ IT network, software quality and integrity

D

> ➤ Restricting your response to the SUBJECT [inventory control system in this case] apply the OBJECTIVES:
>
>   i.   Risks
>   ii. Controls
> ➤ Ensure that you apply sufficient theory and tools to earn the available marks. Usually, 2 marks per CORRECT and APPROPRIATE fact/tool/methodology applied.

SUMMARY OF FACTS KNOWN ABOUT THE SUBJECT:

Inventory control system.

   [i.e. What can we determine from the information given in the question regarding the inventory control system?]

Continues . . .

> "‥ buys and sells small electronic components …" = hard to track small valuable items that can easily be concealed, miscounted or damaged.

> "‥ sales of $200 million per annum ‥" = even if the COGS is as low as 60% of sales (arbitrary proportion that I applied) then the inventory handled per annum will be $120 million. Their provision for shrinkage is 2% or $2,400,000 – a sizeable sum to lose annually and is (2.4M/12M) 20% of the net profit lost. The benefit of addressing this loss is obvious.

> High level of risk of product obsolescence due to technological changes with little prior warning.

> "Purchasing Manager authorises the disposal of obsolete inventory." – Potential opportunity for the manipulation of poor purchasing decisions within the hands of the originator department.

> "‥ 30,000 different components ‥" high number of different SKUs (stock keeping units) that has to be managed and controlled.

> Manual paper based order placing and goods receipt that is secondary captured into the computer-based system (a software system which is 10 years old and does not integrate all of the input-process-output functions for the management and control of inventory)

> Picking process is used to manipulate computer-based inventory records.

> Annual physical stock take that is used to adjust recorded to physical count and provides the basis for write-offs.

R **Question Two required – Part (b)**

(b) Recommend (without being specific to the CSX scenario) the tests or techniques, both manual and computerised, that internal auditors can use in assessing the adequacy of inventory controls.

A

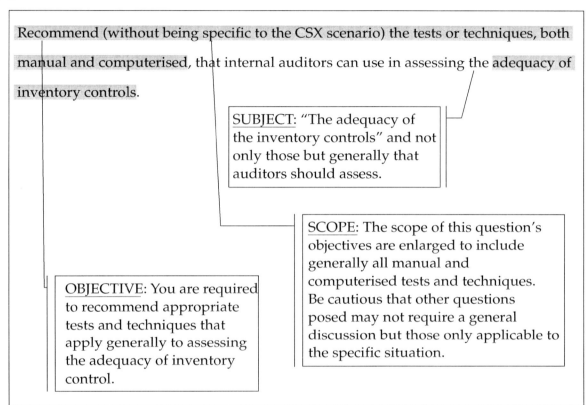

Recommend (without being specific to the CSX scenario) the tests or techniques, both manual and computerised, that internal auditors can use in assessing the adequacy of inventory controls.

SUBJECT: "The adequacy of the inventory controls" and not only those but generally that auditors should assess.

SCOPE: The scope of this question's objectives are enlarged to include generally all manual and computerised tests and techniques. Be cautious that other questions posed may not require a general discussion but those only applicable to the specific situation.

OBJECTIVE: You are required to recommend appropriate tests and techniques that apply generally to assessing the adequacy of inventory control.

I

SUBJECT: adequacy of inventory controls: Define both manual and computerised inventory systems controls to be tested. Ch 6 discusses Internal Controls and lists the controls necessary for inventory management. In addition, the Inventory Management system could include computerized systems. Therefore, the predictive and preventative systems controls that apply to the broad areas of security, integrity and contingency discussed in Ch 9 apply.

OBJECTIVE: Recommend (without being specific to the CSX scenario) the tests or techniques, both manual and computerized: Importantly, the question tests your ability to synthesize the general inventory controls tests and techniques with those applicable to computer-based systems.

Ch 7 (Q7.15) deals with the three principal test techniques that auditors should apply:

➢ Walk-through
➢ Compliance tests
➢ Substantive tests

Continues . . .

You should discuss the practical application of methods and models that internal auditors should deploy (Extracts from Q 7.14)

Ch 9 covers the topic of Information Systems Control Auditing. You should apply those tests and techniques that specifically apply to inventory controls – and NOT to any other area or aspect of the business.

> ➢ Test data using CAAT.
> ➢ Embedded audit facilities
> ➢ SCARF Automated software that monitors transactions and changes
> ➢ Audit interrogation software

D

> ➢ The question requires that you make specific recommendations. Just listing the theory, methods and tests without describing HOW they will deliver a solution to the management objectives will not constitute a recommendation as required.

 The specific facts of the case described in the question do NOT apply to part (b) even though it is located as part of the question. This is an opportunity for you to integrate the general internal auditing tests and methods with those applicable to computerised systems that will demonstrate to the examiner that you have an understanding of the extended requirements and opportunities provided by technology to audit a business function.

Examiner's Answer to May 2008 – Question Two

(a)

The computer system is 10 years old; local managers are unconcerned by the problem but the audit objective set by the Board is to reduce the annual 2% write-off. Given that the company makes an annual profit of 6% ($12 m/$200 m) the annual stock write-off of 2% is a material item for financial reporting and for management action.

(i) Internal controls generally:

The following are the specific risks identified in the scenario (in no particular order of significance) and the following internal control improvements (in italics) could be made in the context of these risks:

- Opportunity for theft of small, high value and readily saleable components by 100 staff operating over 2 shifts. *Improved physical security over warehouse, ensure no access by unauthorised staff, random checks of employees, use of CCTV, checking of items picked for delivery against Delivery Note/Invoice to identify discrepancies. Widespread communication of a fraud response plan within the company.*
- Risk of obsolescence, and obsolete stock being disposed of without proper authorisation and recording. *Disposal of obsolete or damaged stock only after proper authorisation by two managers, under supervision, and with proper recording of obsolete stock write-offs.*
- Lack of separation of duties in Central Warehouse between those handling goods and those doing data entry (different people but in same department under control of same manager). *Separation of data entry staff from Central Warehouse to separate office under different manager.*
- Shortages in goods actually received compared with quantity invoiced by suppliers. *Improved procedure to record receipts. Automated purchase order system with comparison of quantity and price ordered with quantity and price received into stock.*
- Overpayments to suppliers and errors in valuation of goods received due to discrepancies between standard cost based on tender price and price actually invoiced by supplier. *Automated purchase order system and valuation of stock as per IFRS based on actual cost into store.*
- Errors in picking stock and incorrect recording of stock to be delivered on Picking Slip. *Investigation of shortages at time of picking to fill customer order.*
- Taken-for-granted nature of 2% contingency (poor control environment). *Change in control environment through management focus on need for improvement.*
- Absence of physical stocktakes more frequently than annually. Inaccurate cut-offs of purchasing and sales at time of annual physical stocktake. *Periodic counts of physical stock on a cyclical basis, for certain groups of components at different times of the year.*

(ii) Internal controls in relation to IT systems:

The major risk is an out-of-date computer system that may not function effectively. Managers in Central Warehouse believe that stock losses are partially a result of inaccurate data entry. In addition, there likely to be clerical errors in recording receipts on manual Goods Received Notes; and data input errors from Picking Slips.

The following IT control improvements could be made:

- Recruitment, training and supervision of data entry staff and separation of duties are important.

- Logical access controls over inventory records by passwords, timeouts of inactive users, logging of access and so on.
- Separation of duties: data entry staff should be in a different department to the Central Warehouse.
- Input controls should include authorisation of transactions prior to data entry, especially that supplier invoices have been re-calculated, prices are correct against tenders and quantities received as per the Goods Received Note should agree with the supplier invoice. This would be a largely automatic process if purchase ordering was automated.
- Data entry should require password access, there should be on-line validation of inventory codes, mandatory data entry fields, reasonableness checks of quantities and approval of all adjustments to stock quantities, especially write-offs.
- Processing controls may include control totals and balancing between the inventory subsidiary ledger and general ledger records.
- Output controls include transaction listings for review, exception reports (for example negative stock quantities which may indicate errors in data entry of inventory codes), forms control over Picking Slips and the combined Delivery Note/Invoice, suspense accounts for unprocessed transactions and up-to-date distribution lists for reports.
- Network controls must also exist with firewalls, data encryption and anti-virus software to prevent hacking, viruses, computer system malfunction or accidental or deliberate alteration of data.

(b)

Internal audit approach: Tests or techniques – manual

Different tests are used to provide evidence about how a system or process is operating to enable the formation of an opinion about the adequacy of internal controls.

- Walk-through tests could be used to follow a selection of inventory transactions through the system from ordering through receipt to storage and despatch, identifying the process and the existing controls.
- Compliance testing would check whether the existing system controls are operating as intended, for example write-off of obsolete stock.
- Substantive tests are relevant when there are weak controls or when fraud is suspected. Testing is usually based on a sample, for example certain stock items, certain suppliers or customers, certain employees or shifts.
- Analytic review involves gaining a better understanding of the control environment and potential internal control weaknesses through using ratio analysis to identify trends, non-financial performance analysis and benchmarking. Ratios such as inventory turn on groups of inventory items and (non-financial) analysis of stock losses identified from the stocktake by location, supplier, value or type may yield useful information. Benchmarking between different suppliers, between different groups of components or (if possible) with competitors may also be useful. Internal control questionnaires of a wide range of staff involved in purchasing, the central warehouse, despatch and data entry may also result in useful clues.
- The main internal audit methods are likely to be regular physical stock counts; corroboration of stock-in-transit records with suppliers and customers; checking of cut-offs; recalculation of supplier invoices and so on. Narratives and flowcharts of system processes may also be helpful.

Auditing IT systems is particularly important given the reliance on computer systems for inventory control.

- Computer assisted audit techniques (CAATs) may be used. Test data can be used to compare the results of inventory processing through the computer system with manual processing to ensure accurate processing by computer.
- Embedded audit facilities allow for a continuous audit review by, for example, an integrated test facility using a false entity, software code comparison programmes to detect programme changes, and logical path analysis programmes which convert software code into flowcharts.
- Audit interrogation software allows auditors to access the inventory system and check large volumes of data by extracting data from computer files, performing calculations, verifying data and comparing it with management reports, and identifying any items that do not comply with system rules.
- Resident audit software permits real-time auditing by tagging items so they can be selected by the auditor at a later date or copied to a system control and review file (SCARF) for later analysis.

RISK & CONTROL

May 2008 – Question Three

LXY is a company, which has a five-year contract to operate buses in and out of the city bus station in Danon, France. The station has 60 bus piers and an average of 90 buses per hour leave Danon for local and national destinations.

Services operate between 06.00 and 22.00 daily. All buses are operated solely by the driver, who loads and unloads luggage and checks that all passengers have a valid ticket. LXY only permits travel with a pre-paid ticket.

Local buses provide a suburban service to areas within a 20 kilometre radius of Danon. The national services cover distances of up to 500 kilometres and so drivers are frequently required to stay overnight at certain destinations before covering the return service the following day.

Requirements

(a) You have recently been appointed Head of Risk and Internal Audit at LXY.

(i) Identify, with a brief justification, three categories which may be used to classify and manage the risks faced by LXY.

(3 marks)

(ii) For ONE of the categories that you have selected in (i) above, identify three possible risks and recommend appropriate tools for their control.

(9 marks)

(Total for Part (a) = 12 marks)

(b) A café owner in Danon has approached LXY with a proposal to provide food and drink facilities on board long-distance bus services.

Identify the additional risks that need to be considered by LXY in the evaluation of the proposal, and how they might be managed.

(4 marks)

(c) Many companies are too small to justify the existence of separate risk management and internal audit functions.

Briefly explain the distinctive roles performed by each of these functions and recommend ways of maintaining their separate effectiveness within a combined department.

(9 marks)

(Total for Question Three = 25 marks)

Response Preparation Suggestions May 2008 – Question Three

$\mathcal{R}$ Question Three required – Part (a - i)

(a) You have recently been appointed Head of Risk and Internal Audit at LXY.

> Note that the appointment of one person to both Risk Management and Internal audit is not considered best practice. For the audit function to be effective, it will be necessary for Internal Auditors to be independent and critical of the Risk Management function as it should be of all functions of the organisation.

(i) Identify, with a brief justification, three categories which may be used to classify and manage the risks faced by LXY.

This response requires recollection of the categories provided in the learning system. See Ch 5 (Q 5.1 or 5.12 or 5.13).

$\mathcal{R}$ Question Three required – Part (a - ii)

(i) For ONE of the categories that you have selected in (i) above, identify three possible risks and recommend appropriate tools for their control.

$\mathcal{A}$

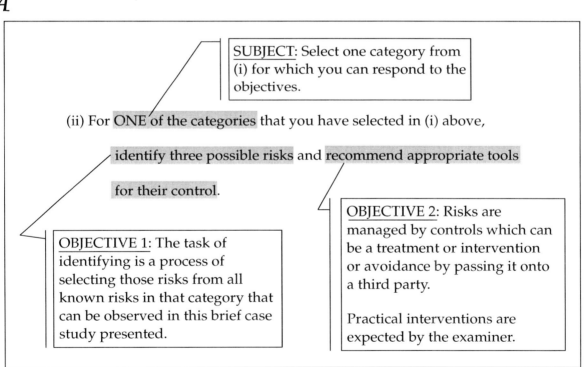

I

> OBJECTIVE 1: identify three possible risks: Three risks falling into the chosen category. Caution should be taken NOT to select risks from differing categories.
>
> OBJECTIVE 2: recommend appropriate tools for their control: This objective tests the student's ability to relate the issue of risk control to the business environment and to detailed interventions, treatment or avoidance of the risks specified.
>
> SUBJECT: Risks (faced by LXY in your chosen category): The task is to list risks in one chosen category that are faced by LXY. Listing across categories will result in lost marks.

D

> ➢ The risks should all be from the one category to earn all of the marks.
>
> ➢ The appropriate controls for each should be presented.

R **Question Three required – Part (b)**

(b) A café owner in Danon has approached LXY with a proposal to provide food and drink facilities on board long-distance bus services.

Identify the additional risks that need to be considered by LXY in the evaluation of the proposal, and how they might be managed.

A

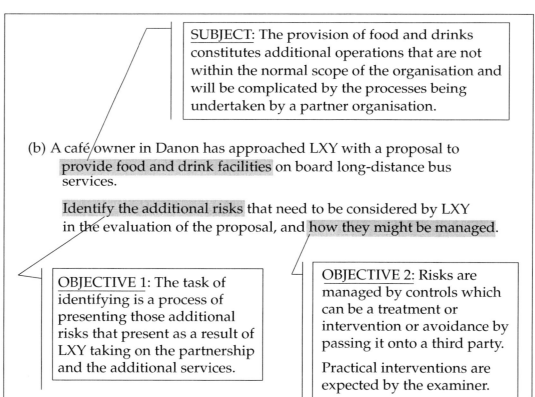

SUBJECT: The provision of food and drinks constitutes additional operations that are not within the normal scope of the organisation and will be complicated by the processes being undertaken by a partner organisation.

(b) A café owner in Danon has approached LXY with a proposal to provide food and drink facilities on board long-distance bus services.

Identify the additional risks that need to be considered by LXY in the evaluation of the proposal, and how they might be managed.

OBJECTIVE 1: The task of identifying is a process of presenting those additional risks that present as a result of LXY taking on the partnership and the additional services.

OBJECTIVE 2: Risks are managed by controls which can be a treatment or intervention or avoidance by passing it onto a third party.

Practical interventions are expected by the examiner.

I

> OBJECTIVE 1: Identify the additional risks: Practical appreciation of the extended business operations and the related additional risks that result.
>
> OBJECTIVE 2: how they might be managed: This objective tests the student's ability to relate the issue of risk control to the business environment and to detailed interventions, treatment or avoidance of the risks specified.
>
> SUBJECT: provide food and drink facilities: This constitutes taking on the additional complications of a partnership and new operations. In practice, a formal iterative process (as described in Q5.30 for example) would be deployed to identify and manage the additional risks associated with taking on a partnership and additional operations. For the purposes of this question, a limited number of risks should simply be identified. The examiner will be testing your ability to practically identify some additional risks that are not associated with the existing operations.

D

> ➢ Marks are given for new risks that are not common to the existing and new operations. The examiner awards marks for both the uniqueness of the risks identified, the spread across the categories and the application of relevant and appropriate controls.

> ➢ Marks are lost where students do not distinguish between the risks faced by both of the operations and where the controls presented are not suited to or best practice for treating the risk.

R Question Three required – Part (c)

(c) Many companies are too small to justify the existence of separate risk management and internal audit functions.

Briefly explain the distinctive roles performed by each of these functions and recommend ways of maintaining their separate effectiveness within a combined department.

A

SUBJECT: This statement sets the subject as a departure from best practice. A practical problem is present (company is too small to justify separate departments) and you will be expected to resolve the objectives to overcome the shortcoming.

(c) Many companies are too small to justify the existence of separate risk management and internal audit functions.

Briefly explain the distinctive roles performed by each of these functions and recommend ways of maintaining their separate effectiveness within a combined department.

OBJECTIVE 1: You are required to recall the theory and to detail the uniqueness of each of the functions.

OBJECTIVE 2: The examiner is testing your ability to deploy best practice in dealing with this situation by stating the training, behaviour and regulatory requirements and norms that each function is required to observe and to suggest ways to resolve the conflicts using controls.

I

OBJECTIVE 1: explain the distinctive roles performed by each of these functions: Your knowledge and recollection of the differing roles of both functions (See Ch 4, Ch 5 and Ch 7).

OBJECTIVE 2: recommend ways of maintaining their separate effectiveness: Best practice principles and regulation governing effective controls and management.

SUBJECT: separate risk management and internal audit functions: Your knowledge of corporate governance best practice (Ch 4 and Q 7.17), the requirements for CIMA members to comply with the published ethical guidelines (Q 7.18), the standards for internal audit are laid down by the Financial Reporting Council Institute of Internal Auditors and the importance of impartially auditing the function and process of risk management.

D

> The central issue in this part of the question is the principle of best practice. Marks are earned for identifying the conflicts of interest between the process function of identifying risks and the necessity for independence and impartiality necessary for the internal audit process to function effectively.

> Reference to the requirements for directors to ensure audit of risks as enshrined in the Combined Code (Ch 4), the CIMA Ethical Guidelines (that are a requirement for all CIMA members to know the contents thereof) and the standards for internal audit as laid down by the Financial Reporting Council Institute of Internal Auditors are essential elements of the response that demonstrate to the examiner that, not only have you considered the practical implications but also the regulatory impact for practitioners and management.

Examiner's Answer to May 2008 – Question Three

(a)

(i) There is a wide range of categories that may be selected and so any choices which are both justified and appropriate to the question context are acceptable. The following list is thus indicative rather than prescriptive. There is also an inevitable potential overlap between some categories.

> Regulatory
> Health and Safety
> Financial
> Operational

(ii) The risks and related controls that apply to each of the categories identified in a (i) include:

Regulatory – Risks may arise in relation to driver training and licensing; vehicle maintenance; employer and public liability insurance; health and safety; employment contracts; compliance with maximum loading rules and so on.

Possible controls:

Formal certificated training programmes and refresher courses for drivers; PCB checks for drivers working on school bus routes where appropriate; maintenance of a database of service records and testing information for all vehicles; employment of a team of inspectors responsible for spot checks on loading and ticketing on bus services.

Health and Safety – Risks may arise in relation to emission levels in public areas; non-smoking rules; disabled access both on the bus station and on the buses; driver training; staff and public security; toilet facilities; food and drink facilities within the bus station; fire protection; risk of accident.

Possible controls:

Installation of environmental monitoring equipment to check emission levels on a regular basis; installation of taco graphs on all long distance buses to ensure drivers keep to the legally limited hours; employment of a disabled services liaison officer to ensure ongoing compliance with relevant legislation; employment of security staff to protect members of the public in the bus station and deter thieves; staff training and certification of all staff working in food and drink service areas; employment and full training of cleaning and maintenance staff; compulsory first aid training for certain categories of staff and installation of first aid packs on all buses.

Financial – Risks may arise in relation to ticket sales; salary payments; fuel purchases; vehicle maintenance and other expenses; preparation of financial statements.

Possible controls:

Separation of responsibility for issuing of customer tickets from the role of maintenance of sales records; purchase of fraud protection software; reconciliation of passenger numbers with tickets issued; employment of suitably qualified accounting staff; use of an approved supplier register for all vehicle servicing and fuel; separation of duties for calculation of salaries due and activation of the payments; purchase of insurance against selected risks, for example fire.

Operational – The company faces risks that bus services may not be able to operate as planned due to unforeseen events such as adverse weather conditions, traffic accidents, or staff absences. Additionally, there are risks of events such as passenger illness; driver illness or road accident that may arise while a service is in operation. They may also lose the local contracts for services if services are poorly run and/or regularly late.

Possible controls:
Register of reserve staff who are willing to be called in at short notice in an emergency; formal monitoring of weather conditions and maintenance of roads and piers within the bus station; installation of a radio control service to monitor vehicle locations and road conditions; establishment of a passenger complaint and compensation scheme in the event of service failure.

(b)

The additional risks that need to be taken into account relate to both compliance with health and safety regulations in relation to the sale of food and drink, and also the risk of poor service impacting upon the reputation of the bus company itself. Contract terms need to be carefully defined in order to specify where the responsibility lies in the case of issues such as damage to buses caused by spillages or the illness of passengers as a result of eating food sold by the third party.

(c)

It is quite common for the risk management function to fall within the internal audit department (or vice versa) of an organisation. The roles are, however, distinct, and good governance practice therefore suggests that internal controls should be established to maintain a degree of separation between audit work and risk management work.

Risk management is concerned with the identification, measurement, treatment and establishment of controls to manage risks. In contrast, internal audit is involved in the testing and evaluation of the risk controls. Good governance practice suggests that those who design the controls should not also be involved in testing them.

The role of a risk management function is to act as an advisory and consultancy service to the operational management and through training and development the risk staff should facilitate operational managers to be able to identify risks in their area of work, and devise controls by which to manage them. The risk managers' expertise is invaluable in helping staff to identify risks and opportunities and understand the ways in which different types of risk can be managed, but risk management is a support function, not an operational one.

Standards for internal audit are laid down by the Financial Reporting Council Institute of Internal Auditors and these are used as the basis for audit work and assessment. It should also be standard practice to annually review the scope of work, authority and resources available to internal audit.

One of the easiest ways to ensure there is no conflict of interest between the two functions within a combined department is by, first, ensuring clear demarcation of responsibilities and second, by putting in place separate reporting lines. The staff in risk management will report to a section head who will, in turn, report to the Board of Directors, probably via the Finance Director. In contrast, the Head of Internal Audit will report to the Audit Committee comprising non-executive directors.

Training regimes should also differ for the two groups of staff, so that the distinctiveness of their skills is clearly reinforced. If risk management staff sit Institute of Risk Management examinations and internal audit staff sit Institute of Internal Audit examinations, then they will regard each other as performing quite different, but complementary, roles.

CURRENCY MANAGEMENT

May 2008 – Question Four

A foreign exchange dealer working in a London-based investment bank wishes to take advantage of arbitrage opportunities in the international money markets.

The following data is available relating to interest rates and exchange rates for Australia and the USA:

	US$/£	A$/£
Spot	2. 0254	2. 3180
6 Month Forward	1. 9971	2. 3602

The effective six-month Australian dollar interest rate is 3.32% and the equivalent US$ rate is 3.68%. These rates apply to both borrowing and lending.

Assume that in six months' time the actual exchange rate between sterling and Australian dollars is A$ 2.32/£.

The dealer is authorised to buy or sell up to US$5 million per transaction. The costs for this type of currency trading are charged in sterling at a rate of £3,000 per transaction.

Note: Each currency conversion counts as one transaction.

Requirements:

(a) Calculate the spot and six-month forward cross-rates between the Australian and US dollar.

(4 marks)

(b) Explain the meaning of the term "arbitrage profit" and explain why such profits may be available in the scenario outlined above. (No illustrative calculations are required).

(6 marks)

(c) Calculate the profit available to the dealer from exploiting the opportunity shown above, clearly showing all of your calculations.

(10 marks)

(d) Explain the importance of "trading limits" and "value at risk" as tools for managing the risks within a financial trading operation.

(5 marks)

(Total for Question Four = 25 marks)

Response Preparation Suggestions May 2008 – Question Four

R (a) Calculate the spot and six-month forward cross rates between the Australian and US dollar.

A

> | OBJECTIVE 1: To identify trading opportunities in the A\$/US\$ currency markets. Note that the requirement is to calculate the spot cross rates. | OBJECTIVE 2: The cross rate requirement comes about because both currencies are quoted in terms of GBP which is the Home currency of the trader. |
>
> (a) Calculate the spot and six-month forward cross rates between the Australian and US dollar (cross-rates).
>
> SUBJECT: The subject is the exchange rate between A\$ to US\$. Importantly, exchange rates are a function of markets and are influenced by conditions and changes taking place in differing currency jurisdictions.
>
> The phenomenon is explained using International Fischer.

I

> The formula for the calculation of the cross rates with US\$ base is:
>
> A\$/US\$ cross-rate = (A\$ ÷ £1) × (£1 ÷ US\$) = (A\$ ÷ US\$)

D

Spot: US\$ = (A\$ ÷ US\$) = 2.3180 ÷ 2.0254 = 1.144 A\$

Forward: A\$ = (A\$ ÷ US\$) = 2.3602 ÷ 1.9971 = 1.1818 A\$

 It is always advisable to write down the generic formula and then write down the formula again with the variable and factor amounts to be calculated. In the heat of exams, we are all inclined to make numeric calculation errors. If you record only the answer, and if it is wrong, the examiner is obliged to record a score of 0 marks. If, however, the examiner can see that you understood the question and used the correct formula she may award some marks. If you have recorded the correct formula and entered the correct amounts for each variable and factor, then even more marks may be awarded.

(b) Explain the meaning of the term "arbitrage profit" and explain why such profits may be available in the scenario outlined above. (No illustrative calculations are required).

> OBJECTIVE: The objective comprises both a primary and a secondary component. The primary component is looking for a definition and the secondary element is looking for application to this case.

> SUBJECT: See Ch 12 and Ch 13 for a discussion of the market participant behaviour for speculation, arbitrage and hedging. It is important to understand these behaviours to fully interpret Purchasing Power Parity, foreign exchange risk and fiscal management.

(b) Explain the meaning of the term "arbitrage profit" and explain why such profits may be available in the scenario outlined above. (No illustrative calculations are required).

> SCOPE: The scope of the response is narrowed by the requirement that the answer should be restricted to the circumstances of this case.
> A wider response loses marks.
>
> Also, the examiner has specifically excused the usual requirement for a quantitatively supported answer. If this is not excused in a question, you should offer a calculation because it usually carries a proportion of the marks.

I The only tool available here is the definition of "arbitrage" which you should have memorised. See Ch 12 for the discussion of trading behaviour definitions.

D

To earn full marks, both the definition and a discussion of the specific situation of this case are required.

 The examiner has given a detailed discussion of the expected answer. The examiner is examining if you understand arbitrage as a concept and to determine if you can apply it to this specific application.

R (c) Calculate the profit available to the dealer from exploiting the opportunity shown above, clearly showing all of your calculations.

A

OBJECTIVE: This is straight forward and requires that you memorise the formula for the exam.

SUBJECT: The opportunity referred to is the "arbitrage" opportunity stated in the question. See Ch 12 for details.

(c) Calculate the profit available to the dealer from exploiting the

opportunity shown above, clearly showing all of your calculations.

NOTE: In this case, leaving out the workings will result directly in lost marks because the examiner specifically requires that they are shown.

You are strongly advised to show all of your workings when presenting any numeric answer. If a mistake in calculation, transposition etc. occurs and you have shown your working then the examiner can see and mark those bits that are correct. If you do NOT show your working then the examiner has no choice but to award zero marks.

I Two tools are required here:
1. The formula of calculating interest rate parity.
2. The steps to determining the profit to the dealer.

D

To earn full marks, both the definition and a discussion of the specific situation of this case are required. See Ch 12.

Alternative Solution 1 – Profit taken at the end of the 6 months

Step Zero
First show that there is an arbitrage opportunity.

Interest rate parity suggests that the forward rate F(A\$/US\$) should be

$$\frac{(1 + r_{A\$})}{(1 + r_{US\$})} \times \text{Spot}_{A\$/US\$} = \frac{1.0332}{1.0368} \times 1.144 = A\$1.140/US\$$$

 The actual exchange rate showing all of the decimal points is A\$ 1.140028 and you are advised to calculate with all or at least 8 decimal points.

Hence, interest rate parity does not hold as the implied quoted forward rate is A\$1.1818/US\$. The dollar is overpriced in the forward market so an arbitrage opportunity exists.

Because the Australian dollar is overpriced in the forward market, the dealer will buy Aus dollars today and sell Australian dollars forward.

Step One
Borrow the equivalent of US\$5 million in Australian dollars.

At the spot rate of A\$1.144/US \$ this equals a loan of A\$5,720,000.

The annualised interest rate of 6.75% equates to a compound rate of 3.32% over six months.

 The examiner has provided the annualised equivalent that is calculated as $((1 + 0.0332)^2 - 1)*100 = 6.75\%$ but you should apply the effective rate for this situation (i.e. 6 months). It is important to apply the correct interest rate to the situation. The actual frequency of compounding that is applicable has a bearing on the calculation. If basis of compounding is not provided, you should state the basis and, even better, provide the calculation showing how you arrived at the effective rate you applied. Also, be very careful to apply all of the decimal values in financial calculations. For example, the actual solution for the annualized interest rate is 6.7502%. In large sums of money, the rounding (of the 0.0002%) can have a significant effect on the final sum of money.

At the end of the period the balance owing is thus A\$ 5,909,904 which is calculated: (US\$ 5,000,000x 1.144) = A\$5,720,000. Then A\$5,720,000 × (1+ 0.0332) = A\$5,909,094.

Step Two
Buy \$5 million US dollars and invest it for six months.

The annualised interest rate of 7.5% equates to a compound rate of 3.68% over six months. $(1+0.0368)^2 - 1 = 7.5\%$

The value at the end of six months is US\$5,000,000 × (1+0.0368) = US\$5,184,000

Step Three
The anticipated US\$ investment receipts are sold forward in exchange for Australian dollars with the intention of using the funds to pay off the loan.

The six-month forward rate is A\$1.1818/US\$.

The sale yields (US\$5,184,000 × 1.1818) = A\$ 6,126,451.

After paying off the loan of A\$5,909,904 this leaves A\$216,547 before costs. The sterling value is £93,339 at the six month spot rate of A\$ 2.32/£, which after costs of £9,000 (3 transactions @ £3000 per transaction) gives a net profit of £84,339 receivable in 6 months time.

Alternative Solution 2 – Profit taken at the beginning of the process

An alternative approach is as follows. This calculation assumes that the trader will take her profits today and not after the six months.

Step Zero
Same as Alt 1.

Step One
Same as Alt 1.

Step Two
At the forward rate of A$1·1818/US$ we receive US$ 5,000,765 in six months.

The present value of this amount is (US$5,000,765 × 1 ÷ (1+ 0.0368) = US$ 4,823,269 which at today's rate equals A$ 5,517,820.

 It is important to remember that the reciprocal of an increment of an amount is $1 \div (1+ r)$.

Thus, the trader buys US$ 4,823,269 [paying in £ sterling] and invests it for six months.

The annualised interest rate of 7·5% equates to a compound rate of 3·68% over six months. The value at the end of six months is (US$4,823,269 × 1.0368) = US$ 5,000,765

Step Three
The anticipated investment receipts are sold forward in exchange for Australian dollars with the intention of using the funds to pay off the loan and interest.

The six-month forward rate is A$1·1818/US$.

The sale of US$ 5,000,765 yields (US$5,000,765 × 1.1818) = A$ 5,909,904 which pays off the loan.

The arbitrage gain is the difference between the amount of A$ borrowed and the cost of the US dollar which equals A$ 202,180 (A$5,720,000 − 5,517,820) [calculated as US$4,823,269 invested at the equivalent of A$ today that is calculated using the spot exchange rate A$ 1.144/US$].

The sterling value of this amount is A$202,180 /2·3180 = £87,222, which after costs of £9,000 gives a net profit of £78,222 today.

(d) Explain the importance of "trading limits" and "value at risk" as tools for managing the risks within a financial trading operation.

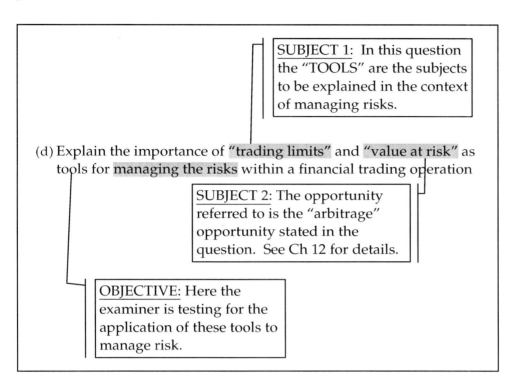

I The definitions and risk control attributes of "trading limits" and "value at risk" are course concepts that should be memorized.

D

In drafting the answer to this question, the following should be borne in mind:
➢ The scope of the risk control.
➢ The limits of the control's scope.
➢ The synergistic or complementary "tools" that, when combined, are effective at providing the control limits desired.

In this question the examiner is exploring your knowledge of the effects and scope of setting trading limits and what the manager is attempting to achieve. On its own, trading limits do not provide a effective cap on the risk in total. It provides for an entry control only. Combined with value-at-risk analysis, the overall risk can be determined and, by so doing, the incidence of taking on and sustaining a high risk exposure can be controlled. At the same time, the manager has to be aware that by setting an upper limit for individual trades, the entire team will be automatically excluded from larger trades. This would automatically exclude the organisation from those larger opportunities. So, for example, setting escalation policies can be a way of overcoming these trade size limits where potential opportunities may beckon.

Examiner's Answer to May 2008 – Question Four

(a)

> Spot: US$ = 1.144 A$
> Forward: US$ = 1.1818 A$

(b)

Arbitrage profit arises when a trader is able to take advantage of price or rating differences between two markets. Arbitrage opportunities will frequently be very short-term in nature because the law of supply and demand ensures that they will disappear automatically as they are taken up. The price of the undervalued item will rise and conversely the price of the overvalued item will fall, until equilibrium is regained.

In the scenario in question there is scope for an arbitrage profit to be earned because the difference in the interest rates in Australia and the USA is not fully reflected in the forward exchange rates. This creates the opportunity to earn a profit by mirroring a money market hedge and borrowing in one currency whilst investing in another for a fixed period of time.

(c)

Step Zero
First show that there is an arbitrage opportunity.

Interest rate parity suggests that the forward rate F(A$/US$) should be

$$\frac{(1+r_{A\$})}{(1+r_{US\$})} \times Spot_{A\$/US\$} = \frac{1.0332}{1.0368} \times 1.144 = A\$1.140/US\$$$

Hence, interest rate parity does not hold as the implied quoted forward rate is A$1.1818/ US$. The dollar is overpriced in the forward market so an arbitrage opportunity exists.

Because the dollar is overpriced in the forward market, the dealer will buy dollars today and sell dollars forward.

Step One
Borrow the equivalent of US $5 million in Australian dollars.

At the spot rate of A$1.144/US $ this equals a loan of A$5,720,000.

The annualised interest rate of 6.75% equates to a compound rate of 3.32% over six months.

At the end of the period the balance owing is thus A$ 5,909,904.

Step Two
Buy $5 million US dollars and invest it for six months.

The annualised interest rate of 7.5% equates to a compound rate of 3.68% over six months.

The value at the end of six months is US$ 5,184,000.

Step Three
The anticipated investment receipts are sold forward in exchange for Australian dollars with the intention of using the funds to pay off the loan.

The six-month forward rate is Aus$1.1818/US$.

The sale yields A$ 6,126,451.

After paying off the loan of A$5,909,904 this leaves A$216,547 before costs. The sterling value is £93,339 at the six-month spot rate of A$ 2.32/£, which after costs of £9,000 gives a net profit of £84,339.

An alternative approach is as follows. This calculation assumes that the trader will take her profits today and not after the six months.

Step Zero
First show that there is an arbitrage opportunity.

Interest rate parity suggests that the forward rate F(A$/US$) should be

$$\frac{(1 + r_{A\$})}{(1 + r_{US\$})} \times \text{Spot}_{A\$/US\$} = \frac{1.0332}{1.0368} \times 1.144 = A\$1.140/US\$$$

Hence, interest rate parity does not hold as the implied quoted forward rate is A$1·1818/US$. The dollar is overpriced in the forward market so an arbitrage opportunity exists.

Because the dollar is overpriced in the forward market, the dealer will buy dollars today and sell dollars forward.

Step One
Borrow the equivalent of US$5 million in Australian dollars.

At the spot rate of A$1·144/US$ this equals a loan of A$5,720,000.

The annualised interest rate of 6·75% equates to a compound rate of 3·32% over six months.

At the end of the period the balance owing is thus A$ 5,909,904.

Step Two
At the forward rate of A$1·1818/US$ we US$ 5,000,765 in six months.

The present value of this amount is US$ 4,823,269 which at today's rate equals A$ 5,517,820.

Thus buy US$ 4,823,269 and invest it for six months.

The annualised interest rate of 7·5% equates to a compound rate of 3·68% over six months. The value at the end of six months is US$ 5,000,765.

Step Three
The anticipated investment receipts are sold forward in exchange for Australian dollars with the intention of using the funds to pay off the loan and interest.

The six-month forward rate is A$1·1818/US$.

The sale of US$ 5,000,765 yields A$ 5,909,904 which pays off the loan.

The arbitrage gain is the difference between the amount of Australian dollar borrowed and the cost of the US dollar which equals A$ 202,180 (5,720,000 − 5,517,820).

The sterling value of this amount is 202,180 /2·3180 = £87,222, which after costs of £9,000 gives a net profit of £78,222 today.

(d)

In the scenario the trader is subject to a monetary limit on the size of the trade that may be conducted. If all dealers on a trading floor are restricted in this way, then the institution can set a cap on the level of its nominal exposure from trading operations. Such monetary limits, however, only relate to the initial size of a transaction and the trader may, for example purchase a future on which margin payments are required to be made, and these may add to the overall risk exposure. At the same time, the trading limit simply restricts the monetary size of an individual transaction but the control does not consider the related portfolio risk of that transaction. A single trade may, for example, increase a company's exposure to the US dollar : sterling exchange rates, but if another trader holds exposure in the opposite direction then the two transactions are naturally hedged.

Value at risk complements the role of trading limits by requiring an evaluation of the potential loss that may be incurred on a whole portfolio, over a set time frame and subject to a pre-defined confidence limit. For example, a one day VaR of £200 million with a 99% confidence limit indicates that there is just a one per cent chance of losses on the portfolio exceeding £200 million within a single 24 hour period. The problem with VaR is that it can be subject to gaming, which occurs when traders take on positions which, at the individual level, are extremely risky and have a high potential pay-off, but nonetheless have a very small impact of the VaR of the overall portfolio. In such cases, the VaR is effectively under-estimating the risk exposure of the business and hence is limited in its control effectiveness.

In conclusion, it is therefore essential to apply a range of different types of control to ensure effective risk management within a trading operation. The controls may be both quantitative and qualitative in nature.

TREASURY MANAGEMENT & CORPORATE GOVERNANCE

May 2008 – Question Five

(a) With specific reference to risk management:

(i) Define and discuss the role of the Treasury function within an organisation.

and

(6 marks)

(ii) Discuss the arguments for and against operating a Treasury function as a profit centre.

(6 marks)
(Total for Part (a) = 12 marks)

(b) Explain the factors a Board of Directors should consider when deciding what to include in the section entitled "Risk Exposure and Control Systems", in their company's report.

(13 marks)
(Total for Question Five = 25 marks)

REMEMBER SENSITIVITY of INFORMATION

R (a) With specific reference to risk management:

(i) Define and discuss the role of the Treasury function within an organisation.

A

FOCUS: The response required should be focused on the particular aspect of risk management to the exclusion of all other perspectives.

(a) With specific reference to risk management:

(i) Define and discuss the role of the Treasury function within an organisation;

OBJECTIVE: The definition of the Treasury function forms part of the content that should be memorised for the module. The examiner requires that the definition be recalled AND discussed – in terms of risk management – and not in general terms.

SUBJECT: The role of the Treasury function within the organisation is discussed in Ch 3.

I Recall of risk management issues and definition of the Treasury function.

Discussion of how the Treasury function can contribute to the risk management and controls programmes. To this end, the examiner has set out various treasury activities that are acceptable as responses to the question. Be cautious to restrict the discussion to the Treasury function.

 It is possible that the opposite can be the basis of such a question where the examiner asks how risk management and management controls should be deployed to ensure effective treasury activities. The "profit centre" question is one way of asking how risk management is brought to bear on the Treasury function. Risk management and controls is an organisation-wide activity in which there is reciprocity of acting upon other functions while others act upon your function.

 (a) With specific reference to risk management:

   (ii) Discuss the arguments for and against operating a Treasury function as a profit centre.

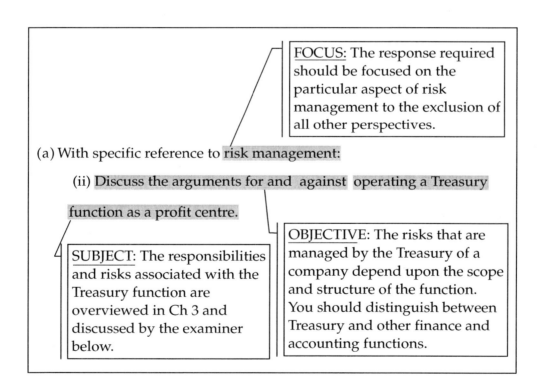

FOCUS: The response required should be focused on the particular aspect of risk management to the exclusion of all other perspectives.

(a) With specific reference to risk management:

   (ii) Discuss the arguments for and against operating a Treasury function as a profit centre.

SUBJECT: The responsibilities and risks associated with the Treasury function are overviewed in Ch 3 and discussed by the examiner below.

OBJECTIVE: The risks that are managed by the Treasury of a company depend upon the scope and structure of the function. You should distinguish between Treasury and other finance and accounting functions.

I The extent of the "tools" applicable can range from management controls, fraud management, efficiency, reward policies, application of corporate governance best practice and the risks associated with market trading that, based upon the profit motive associated therewith, introduces both advantages and disadvantages.

D The examiner is testing to see if you are able to discuss and contrast the benefits of motivating the Treasury team by structuring and remunerating the function as a profit centre. Benefits include the performance of trades in the market, potential for the reduction of the cost of capital and investment returns improved based upon performance related remuneration and incentives. By contrast the market risks, internal controls, fraud potential and internal competition for cash resources require specific management.

R (b)   Explain the factors a Board of Directors should consider when deciding what to include in the section entitled "Risk Exposure and Control Systems", in their company's report.

A

> OBJECTIVE: The range of factors should be extracted from the relevant sections of the Combined Code, GAAP (FRS7) and FRC report. In particular, compliance with minimum reporting requirements have to be balanced against disclosing details related to operating tactics and strategic financial positioning.

(b) Explain the factors a Board of Directors should consider when deciding what to include in the section entitled "Risk Exposure and Control Systems", in their company's report.

> SUBJECT: The reporting requirements and disclosures associated with the Combined Code, FRS (particularly FRS 7), the compliance with the requirement for a business review as part of the Directors' Report and the issues raised by the Financial Reporting Council should all be considered in terms of reporting under this heading.
>
> The examiner has provided a concise discussion of the topic and you are referred to the codes, GAAP and FRC for further study.

I A broad knowledge of the Combined Code; GAAP with particular focus on FRS 7; Financial Reporting Council report 2008 and London Stock Exchange rules is required.

D The examiner has demonstrated the range and depth of the answer required. The approach taken is practical and draws from the risks and controls associated with the module, the legislative framework and codes of conduct with which the directors of the company are obligated to comply and with which the student is expected to be familiar.

Examiner's Answer to May 2008 – Question Five

(a) (i)

The Treasury function within an organisation is responsible for management of the funding and investment areas of the business, including hedging of financial risks.

The debt : equity mix, the ratio of long-term to short-term borrowing, and the level of exposure to fixed versus variable interest rates all create financial risks which must be managed within the confines of the risk appetite specified by the Board of Directors. It is the responsibility of the Treasury division to identify suitable sources of funding, obtain quotes for loan finance, and appoint bankers to manage equity issues as appropriate. Effective control of borrowing and investment activity requires that Treasury staff are fully aware of operational cash flows and thus able to budget for future cash requirements. Treasury will also commonly take responsibility for the evaluation of projects within the organisation and the production of rankings based upon the financial dimensions of the project.

In addition to arranging sources of funds, Treasury staff are also involved in identifying investment opportunities to make effective use of surplus short-term cash positions. This may involve overnight lending or the purchase of commercial paper or Treasury notes as short-term investments. The distribution of dividend payments is also a Treasury responsibility although the decision on the size of the dividend is not part of its remit. In making these short-term investments, close attention must be paid to the associated levels of risk.

(ii)

The management of financial risks arising from exposure to interest rate and currency movements is a core element of the Treasury function. Where Treasury services are centralised, the risks from the separate divisions within a business will be internally netted and decisions taken on the extent to which the residual risk will be hedged via external means. The transaction costs arising from external hedging may vary and so another requirement is that Treasury understands and compares the relative costs of alternative hedging methods.

The level of hedging that is undertaken reflects the willingness of the business to tolerate a given level of financial risk, or accept the cost of protection through hedging. In a significant proportion of businesses Treasury is seen as a cost centre, the performance of which is evaluated in terms of the management of costs relative to prescribed targets. It is also possible, however, for Treasury to be run as a profit centre. In such cases, performance is evaluated in terms of the ability of Treasury staff to use surplus funds to generate additional profit for the organisation. The cost centre approach is risk averse, while the profit centre approach is risk taking.

One relevant factor in the decision is the extent to which Treasury is viewed as servicing the needs of the rest of the business or as a business in its own right. In the case of companies such as Enron, the trading operations became larger than the underlying business, and it is clear that Treasury was not really acting as a service centre. The financial speculation proved to be one element in the company's downfall in Enron's case, but this does not imply that using Treasury to earn profits is bad per se.

There is no definitively "correct" approach to Treasury management because the decision to opt for a cost or profit based style is ultimately dependent upon the risk appetite of the organisation, as established by the Board of Directors. Operating as a cost centre offers the advantage that there is no risk of large losses arising from speculative activity that may wipe out profits from ordinary business activities. Conversely, treating it as a cost centre may involve ignoring highly lucrative potential opportunities in the financial markets which could increase overall profits. The decision on which approach to adopt must be left with the Board.

(b)

Until recently, the extent to which a listed company is required to report to external parties on the nature and extent of its exposures to business risks and the methods used to manage those risks has been the subject of minimal regulatory control. In certain specific areas, such as financial instruments, there have been well defined requirements (see for example IAS 39, IFRS 7 and SFAS 133) on what should be reported, but less explicit advice on how to report for example qualitative versus quantitative reporting.

In the UK compliance with the Combined Code requires the publication of a governance report which includes information on the structures in place for risk management and control. Additionally, legislation was introduced in 2005 which required the inclusion of a business review within the Directors' Report. The legislation does not explicitly require the inclusion of risk and control information within the business review although it more broadly states that from October 2008 it should include information on the main trends likely to affect the future development, performance and position of the company's business. Intuitively, one might expect this to incorporate information about key risks and their management.

A report published in January 2007 by the Financial Reporting Council on current trends in narrative reporting practice concluded that there was evidence of weaknesses in the reporting of key risks and uncertainties. This suggests that current risk reporting practice focuses on the governance procedures and control systems rather than on the provision of information about the risks themselves.

This approach probably reflects the view that revealing data on risks may be commercially sensitive and may also be misunderstood by the users of the annual report. Furthermore, it can be argued that if a company can provide evidence of a robust system of internal controls, then investors can reasonably assume that any risks that may be encountered will be reasonably well managed. This requires the reader to place faith in the systems, even though there is no requirement in the regulations for directors to report on the effectiveness of the internal control system. They are merely required to report that the systems have been reviewed on an annual basis.

In deciding what, and how much to report about risks and the systems for their management, a company must pay attention to the sensitivity and potential complexity of such information. Ultimately, it can be argued that risk reporting is itself a risk that has to be managed, and it is for this reason that remains very wide variations in current practice.

FOREIGN EXCHANGE & INTEREST RATE MANGAGEMENT

November 2007 – Question Two (Changed for learning purposes)

X is a small company based in England. The company had the choice of launching a new product in either England or France but lack of funding meant that it could not do both. The company bases its decisions on Expected Net Present Value (ENPV) and current exchange rates. As a result of this methodology, and the details shown below, it was decided to launch in England (with an ENPV of £28,392) and not France (with an ENPV of £25,560).

		England Probability		France Probability
Launch Costs			**Launch Costs**	
£145,000	0·1		£190,000	1·0
£120,000	0·9			
Annual Cash Flows			**Annual Cash Flows**	
£65,000	0·4		£90,000	0·5
£42,000	0·4		£70,000	0·2
£24,000	0·2		£30,000	0·3

The annual cash flows are based on contribution margins of 10% for England and 20% for France where it is expected that sales volumes will be lower. It is thought that the product will sell for four years only.

The monetary values are expressed in the home currency of the company and have been converted (where necessary) at the current exchange rate of €1.47/£1.

The company has discounted the cash flows using a cost of capital of 10% per year.

Requirements

(a) It has now been forecast that the Euro is likely to strengthen against sterling by 5% in each of the next four years.

Calculate and briefly comment upon the revised Expected Net Present Value if the product is launched in France.

(5 marks)

(b) Identify the different risks associated with each launch option and discuss how these may be managed by the company.

(8 marks)

(Total for requirements (a) and (b) = 13 marks)

(c) Company X wishes to raise a £500,000 fixed rate bank loan to fund the product launch and additional capital investments. Company X is able to obtain fixed rate finance at 8·5% or a variable rate loan at LIBOR + 0·5%. Using its bank as an intermediary, Company X has been offered a swap arrangement with HTM, a smaller company that wishes to borrow at a fixed rate. HTM has been quoted a rate of 10·5% for a fixed rate loan or LIBOR + 1·1% for a floating rate loan. The bank charge for arranging a swap is 0·2% of the principal, and it is assumed that the net benefits will be shared equally between Company X and HTM.

Requirements

(i)   Briefly discuss the potential benefits and hazards of interest rate swaps as a tool for managing interest rate risk.

(6 marks)

(ii) Show the transactions involved, the bank charges and the interest terms payable if X and HTM agree to the swap.

(6 marks)
(Total for requirement (c) = 12 marks)
(Total for Question Two = 25 marks)

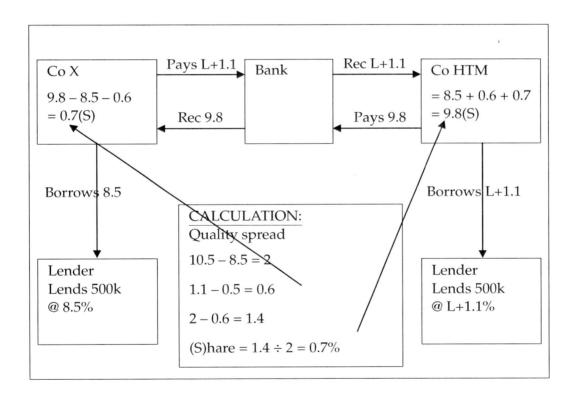

Examiner's Answer to November 2007 – Question Two

(a)

France Launch: Revised ENPV

Expected cost	= £190,000
Forecast cash flows	*PV*
Year 1: £71,400	£64,903
Year 2: £74,970	£61,925
Year 3: £78,718	£59,117
Year 4: £82,654	£56,453
	£242,398
NPV = £242,398 − £190,000 =	£52,398

The adjustment of cash flows to reflect the strengthening of the Euro substantially increases the NPV generated by a launch in France and reverses the decision made on the basis of X's original methodology. This reversal indicates the potential sensitivity of present values to changes in the key assumptions, and specifically the exchange rates used in the calculation of overseas cash flows.

(b)

There are two types of risks faced by X in making its launch decision. The first set of risks relate to the market conditions, strategic implications and cash flow risks of the two alternative locations. The second set of risks relates to the limitations of the methodology chosen for decision-making.

The risks associated with expanding overseas are very different to the risks of focusing on the domestic market. There are issues of cultural understanding, language, exchange rate risk, and broader market knowledge that all need to be taken into account in the decision process. Some of these risks can be reduced by additional market research and changes in company strategy such as the use of a joint venture arrangement. Others may be more difficult to eradicate and the potential threat they pose to cash flows needs to be incorporated into decision-making.

By launching in the UK rather than France, X 's decision ignores the broader strategic considerations, and their associated risks, with the result that the company forfeits potential expansion opportunities. These opportunities may not appear financially viable over the time frame used for the investment decision, but may be important for the long-term development of the business. In the absence of additional information, if X is assumed to be a UK-based company, then a UK launch simply means that it is expanding its position within the domestic market place. This may bring good short term growth levels for the business, but may not offer the longer-term potential of a move into Europe, which could open up a significant range of new opportunities. Control of strategic risks can be achieved by ensuring that such considerations form a part of all major investment decisions.

In purely financial terms France seems to pose less risk because the launch costs appear certain, but this is not actually true in reality. There is a risk that the exchange rate will change between the date of the decision and the date at which the costs are incurred, but this could be managed relatively easily by the use of a forward contract that would fix the exchange rate.

The exchange rate risk extends to affect the cash flows throughout the life of the product. As the solution to (a) demonstrated, even a small change in the exchange rate can reverse the project rankings in terms of their ENPV. The risk can be better understood via the application of sensitivity analysis on the NPV using different exchange rate scenarios, and the resulting exchange rate uncertainties can be managed via the use of a range of different hedging tools. These may include both internal and external hedging, such as netting, forward contracts, futures, or currency swaps. The exchange rate risk implicit in the launch in France may be regarded as significantly affecting the project's risk profile relative to the UK launch, and consideration must be given as to whether this additional risk is acceptable to the Board of Directors.

The relative risk for the UK is that the contribution margin is comparatively low, which leaves limited scope for price cutting if the launch is not successful. This is counterbalanced by the fact that the probability schedule indicates that higher rather than lower sales levels are the most likely, but even these are not certain. The risk of low margins can be managed by detailed market research to evaluate the price elasticity of demand for the product. It may be that the net contribution could be increased by raising prices (and margins) in combination with lower sales volumes.

One possible approach to dealing with different levels of risk across projects would be to adopt different discount rates with a higher rate being applied to the project perceived as carrying the greater expected risks. This method creates a problem insofar as each additional risk has to be allocated a value in terms of a discount rate adjustment and this requires the use of subjective judgement. Additionally, a discount rate adjustment may not be necessary for some of the risks, such as exchange rate volatility because these may be managed via the use of hedging tools.

An alternative approach, as used in this case, is to use a common discount rate for both France and the UK. The final choice is then made by subjectively comparing the resulting ENPVs. Making this type of judgement is also difficult, however, because the ENPV for the UK is just £2,832 higher than that for France.

In terms of the methodology, there are problems with both the computation of the ENPV and also the emphasis that is placed upon just the financial dimensions of the decision. The NPV calculations are based on expected costs and expected contribution levels. In practice it is unlikely that the expected values will ever be realised, which means that there is a possibility that the ENPV for the UK may actually be lower than expected or even lower than in France. Furthermore, the cash flow forecasts are based upon just four years of data, whilst the effective product life may be much longer. As a result, the decision may be based upon incomplete information.

The key problem for X is that the criteria used for decision making are purely financial in nature, and as a result they ignore all of the non financial elements that may affect this type of strategic decision. Ideally, investments should be based upon a blend of both financial and non financial factors, which accurately reflect the risk appetite of the company's Board of Directors.

(c) (i)

Interest rate swaps are a useful tool for the management of interest rate risk because they allow a company to switch between fixed and variable rate loans, and therefore take a position on the future direction of interest rates. For example, a company may believe that interest rates have "bottomed out" and hence choose to swap its variable rate loans for fixed rate ones set at the current low interest rate level. In making this swap, the company is affirming its belief that future rates will rise ie taking a position.

In many but not all cases, swaps are used to obtain funding at a lower rate than that available elsewhere, but they can also be used beneficially to manage future cash flow patterns. If, for example, a company is operating in a market where its incoming cash flows are uncertain, it may wish to use a swap to ensure that it has fixed rate commitments that are wholly predictable. In so doing, it minimises uncertainty of outgoings even if it cannot eliminate the uncertainty in respect of incoming cash.

Interest rate swaps may also be used to manage interest rate risk in respect of investments rather than borrowings. In such cases a swap may be useful in enhancing the returns via speculation on interest rate movements. One such example would be a decision to swap a variable rate for a fixed rate investment in the belief that interest rates will fall.

A key advantage of interest rate swaps is that because they are an over the counter product, they can be tailored to meet the specific needs of the company, in terms of both their duration and value. Where the swap is arranged without the use of an intermediary, transaction costs are also kept to a minimum, although this also results in a disadvantage because it creates a counterparty credit risk. In the absence of an intermediary, there is no guarantee that the counterparty will fulfil their part of the contract, although this credit risk can be minimised by seeking a credit rating on the counterparty before agreeing to a swap.

Another disadvantage of swap arrangements is that the binding nature of the agreement means that a company may find itself unable to take advantage of changing interest rates that move in its favour. This problem is reinforced by the lack of a secondary market for swaps which means that it is difficult if not impossible to liquidate a contract.

(ii)

The quality spread differential is 1·4% before bank charges.

HTM has a comparative advantage in the floating rate market and Company X has a comparative advantage in the fixed rate market. X therefore borrows at 8·5% fixed, and HTM borrows at LIBOR plus 1·1% floating.

Workings

X		HTM	
Borrows at	8·5%	Borrows at	LIBOR + 1·1 %
Receives from HTM	9·8%	Receives	LIBOR + 1·1%
Pays to HTM	LIBOR + 1·1 %	Pays to X	9·8%
Net interest cost (before charges)	LIBOR + 0·21%	Net interest cost (before charges)	10·1% fixed

For Company X there is a net saving of 0·4% over the floating rate of LIBOR + 0·5% that it would otherwise have to pay. The net gain is computed as follows:

Fixed rates: Pays 8·5% but receives 9·8 % giving a gain of 1·3%
Floating rates: Pays LIBOR + 1·1 % against available rate of LIBOR + 0·5%, giving an opportunity loss of 0·6%.
Net gain (before charges) 1·3 % *less* **0·**6% = **0·**7%

For HTM there is a net saving of 0·4% over the fixed rate of 10·5% that it would otherwise have to pay for a fixed rate loan. The net gain is computed as follows:

Floating rate: Pays LIBOR + 1·1% and receives LIBOR + 1·1 %, giving a gain of zero. Fixed Rate: Pays 9·8 % against an available rate of 10·5% giving an opportunity gain of 0·7 %.
Net gain = **0·**7%

In total, the net gain of 1·4% that is shared between the two parties is exactly equal to the quality spread differential. The bank charge of 0·2% of the £500,000 principal equals £1,000 and this cost is also shared equally.

INTERNAL CONTROLS (A); IT SYSTEMS CONTROLS (B); FRAUD (C)

November 2007 – Question Three
VWS is a company manufacturing and selling a wide range of industrial products to a large number of businesses throughout the country. VWS is a significant local employer, with 2,500 people working out of several locations around the region, all linked by a networked computer system.

VWS purchases numerous components from 750 local and regional suppliers, receiving these components into a central warehouse. The company carries about 10,000 different inventory items, placing 25,000 orders with its suppliers each year.

The Accounts Payable Department of VWS has six staff who process all supplier invoices through the company's computer system and make payment to suppliers by cheque or electronic remittance.

Requirements

(a) Discuss the purposes and value of an internal control system for Accounts Payable to a company like VWS.

(10 marks)

(b) Identify the information systems controls that should be in place for Accounts Payable in a company like VWS.

(10 marks)

(c) Explain the risk of fraud in a computerised Accounts Payable system for a company like VWS and how that risk can be mitigated.

(5 marks)
(Total for Question Three = 25 marks)

(a) Discuss the purposes and value of an internal control system for Accounts Payable to a company like VWS.

A

> OBJECTIVE: Be cautious not to only describe the purposes of internal controls but to describe the value to the organisation.
>
> SUBJECT: See Ch 6 read with 1, 2 and 5. The examiner is testing for your ability to identify those internal controls that relate to Accounts Payable and NOT to describe the purposes of internal controls generally.
>
> (a) Discuss the purposes and value of an internal control system for Accounts Payable to a company like VWS.
>
> FOCUS: Be sure to address only those internal controls applicable to the narrowing focusing on "Accounts Payable". An answer dealing with internal controls generally without a link to Accounts Payable will lose marks.

I Based upon Policies/Procedures/Practice, extract appropriate internal controls from Ch 6 with reference to Ch 1, 2 and addressing risks detailed in Ch 5 that relate directly to Accounts Payable.

D In addressing this question you should discuss the risks that require controlling in relation to Accounts Payable and relate the appropriate internal controls to those risks. Authorisation, cash management, document management and quantity, quality and specification verification are valid areas for control. The examiner is also looking for the value to be discussed. Bear in mind that all controls carry costs and their implementation should hold benefits for the organisation. Controls address decision-making, financial management, quality and quantity validation and should have feedback mechanism to enable double-loop learning for the organisation.

(b) Identify the information systems controls that should be in place for Accounts Payable in a company like VWS.

OBJECTIVE: This response does not require a discussion but only the identification of IS controls directly related to Accounts Payable.

SUBJECT: The examiner has taken the approach that the system under consideration is a networked situation. You should describe the situation you are dealing with so that the appropriateness of the controls can be assessed properly. See Ch 8 and 9

(b) Identify the information systems controls that should be in place for Accounts Payable in a company like VWS.

FOCUS: Be sure to address only those information systems controls applicable to the narrowing focusing on "Accounts Payable". An answer dealing with information systems controls generally without a link to Accounts Payable will lose marks.

I   The main risks (Q 9.9) addressed by designing input–process–output controls and processes including hardware and software protection, firewalls protecting data, security post words, data encryption supported by embedded audit facilities, audit interrogation software and an appropriate SCARF system are all relevant to the discussion although not all specifically discussed by the examiner below.

D   The examiner has addressed to broad areas namely those general IS controls and specific IS controls related to Accounts Receivable. Generally, the examiner would expect you to discuss an environment representative of a larger corporation where computer networking, separation of duties, the need for data protection due to the exposure to wide area computer networks.

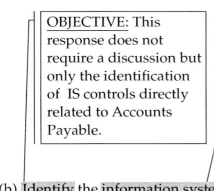   In order to ensure that the examiner can identify the context in which you are answering the question, you should state your assumptions about the situation you are describing.

R (c) Explain the risk of fraud in a computerised Accounts Payable system for a company like VWS and how that risk can be mitigated.

NOTE: This is a five mark question requiring the explanation of one risk and how it can be mitigated.

A

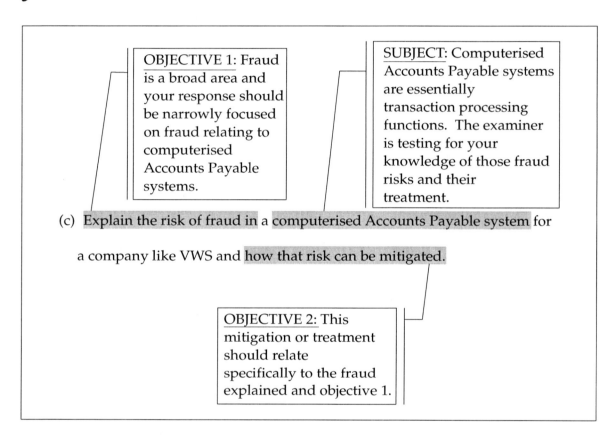

OBJECTIVE 1: Fraud is a broad area and your response should be narrowly focused on fraud relating to computerised Accounts Payable systems.

SUBJECT: Computerised Accounts Payable systems are essentially transaction processing functions. The examiner is testing for your knowledge of those fraud risks and their treatment.

(c) Explain the risk of fraud in a computerised Accounts Payable system for a company like VWS and how that risk can be mitigated.

OBJECTIVE 2: This mitigation or treatment should relate specifically to the fraud explained and objective 1.

I This response should focus on computer-based fraud as discussed in Ch 10 of the learning system.

D Care should be taken to select a specific fraud related to the Accounts Receivable function as processed using computerised information systems and the treatment related to the mitigation of the fraud specifically discussed.

The examiner highlights the importance of control over the program changes, editing data, authorisation processes and security access provisions.

Examiner's Answer to November 2007 – Question Three

(a)

An internal control system comprises the policies and procedures that an organisation implements to achieve its objectives, efficiently and effectively conduct its business, safeguard its assets, prevent and detect fraud, and ensure the accuracy and completeness of accounting records in order to produce reliable financial statements. In relation to Accounts Payable, internal controls ensure that suppliers are paid accurately and on time in order to ensure continuity of supply. Because the payment of money is involved, the safeguarding of cash resources is critical to the Accounts Payable function and the opportunity for fraud by employees or suppliers must be minimised. As the processing of supplier invoices has a material impact on the accuracy of financial statements, approval and end of financial period cut-off procedures need to be effective. The control environment within a company like VWS must be supportive of these controls.

The purposes of controls over Accounts Payable are that:

- purchases are properly authorised through an effective purchase ordering system;
- goods are received or services supplied, and that these are in accordance with that purchase order;
- the price on invoices is checked, and that calculations are correct;
- invoices are properly authorised for payment with supporting evidence;
- invoices are correctly posted to creditor accounts in the accounting period in which goods are received or services provided;
- payments are made to suppliers in accordance with trading terms, are properly authorised and recorded in creditor accounts;
- creditor accounts are regularly reconciled with supplier statements; and
- a thorough investigation of any disputed amounts takes place.

The value of controls may be seen in their functioning as directive, preventative, detective, and corrective. Some controls are directive. Training or policies and procedures show employees what should be done. In Accounts Payable, training and policies would provide the parameters in which the department would carry out the transaction processing of invoices and payment. For example, staff would not be permitted to use the system unless they had been properly trained and were made aware of the Accounts Payable Department's written policies and procedures.

(b)

A number of general controls are particularly important in a distributed information systems environment. Personnel controls cover recruitment, training, supervision and the separation of duties. Physical access controls limit access to computer systems, whilst logical access controls prevent unauthorised access to data through password controls. Business continuity or disaster recovery puts procedures in place to recover physical computer systems and data if a critical business event such as a fire or flood occurs.

In addition, specific input, processing and output controls will apply to each software application. These will include input controls covering transaction authorisation, completeness and accuracy of data entry, on-line code verification, reasonableness checks, and supporting evidence for all adjustments. Processing controls cover standardised coding and processes, control totals, and balancing between subsidiary and general ledgers. Output controls include transaction lists, exception reports, forms control, and suspense accounts.

Network controls in a distributed processing environment provide protection against hacking, viruses and unauthorised access through firewalls, data encryption and virus protection software.

(c)

Computer systems provide a particular opportunity for fraud, although this requires dishonesty by employees, opportunity to commit fraud, and motive. Accounts Payable in particular presents the opportunity for unscrupulous suppliers to claim payment for goods not delivered or services not supplied, or to overcharge. It also provides the opportunity for employees to redirect payments to themselves or third parties rather than to the intended supplier, either alone or in concert with third parties.

Some controls are preventative to limit or prevent an event from occurring. This could include physical access control over the computer system, selection and training of staff, separation of duties between invoice and payment processing or authorisation levels for invoices and payments. Other controls are detective: they identify events that have already occurred, through for example the reconciliation of invoices to a supplier statement. Internal audit, based on risk identification and assessment procedures have an important role to play in detective controls. Finally, corrective controls correct events after they have occurred, e.g. recovering overpayments from suppliers, or seeking recompense from employees under a fraud response plan.

It is particularly important that strong controls exist over programme alterations to accounts payable software, physical and logical access controls to accounts payable systems, authorisation levels for invoices and payments and control over forms such as cheques and electronic bank remittances.

The risk of fraud can be reduced through fraud prevention, identification and response policies. Fraud prevention requires an anti-fraud culture and risk awareness which is part of the control environment, sound control systems, and an effective whistle-blowing policy.

Fraud can be identified through regular internal audit checks, warning signals such as late payments, work backlogs, untaken annual leave, and the lifestyle of staff where it is incommensurate with their salary. Fraud response should include disciplinary action under human resource policies, civil litigation for recovery and criminal prosecution.

RISKS AND CONTROLS

November 2007 – Question Four

EWC is a large company in an unregulated sector of the telecommunications industry. It has ambitious plans for sales growth and increased profitability. In support of these goals, senior management has established a flat management structure. Budget targets place employees under considerable pressure but success in achieving and surpassing sales and profitability targets is rewarded by bonuses and share options. Employees who do not achieve their targets do not remain with the company for long.

Performance targets exist for expanding EWC's customer base, sales value and profitability per customer, and geographic and product-based expansion. EWC zealously pursues cost reduction with continual efforts to drive down suppliers' prices. The company aims to eliminate any wasteful practices in management and administration. EWC considers any expenditure that does not lead directly to sales growth to be wasteful and the company minimises its corporate policies and procedures. As a result, EWC has tended to overlook unscrupulous practices in its employees' dealings with customers, competitors and suppliers in the pursuit of its goals. The company is unlisted and reports its profits to shareholders once per year.

Requirements

(a) Identify the major types of risk facing EWC that arise from its style of management. Give reasons to support your answer.

(10 marks)

(b) Explain the significance of the control environment in EWC.

(5 marks)

(c) From the perspective of a newly appointed non-executive director, evaluate the financial, non-financial quantitative, and qualitative controls in EWC in the context of EWC's goals and the risks facing EWC.

(10 marks)
(Total for Question Four = 25 marks)

R (a) Identify the major types of risk facing EWC that arise from its style of management. Give reasons to support your answer.

A

OBJECTIVE: The specific narrowing to "style of management" as subject requires that the student demonstrate clearly the MAJOR RISK TYPES relative to the specific style of management. Caution should be taken not to offer unrelated or generic type answers because the examiner will interpret that as a distinct lack of knowledge in respect of the application of risk theory.

(a) Identify the major types of risk facing EWC that arise from its

style of management. Give reasons to support your answer.

SUBJECT: The student is required to ascertain the style of management prevailing at the company based upon the perceived behaviour. You are required to deduct the pressuring, aggressive and gung-ho approach of management.

EXTENSION: This extension to the objective enables the examiner to test your ability to justify the identification you have put forward and to confirm your understanding of the application of the theory to the case.

I Management style theory as discussed in Ch 2 of this Practice Kit. The work of Geert Hofstede is important for a fuller understanding of this topic.

D The examiner is looking to determine whether you are able to distinguish differing styles of management and their differing impact upon staff behaviour and response. In his solution, the examiner has provided a flexible approach to acceptable responses allowing for practical experience to prevail.

(b) Explain the significance of the control environment in EWC.

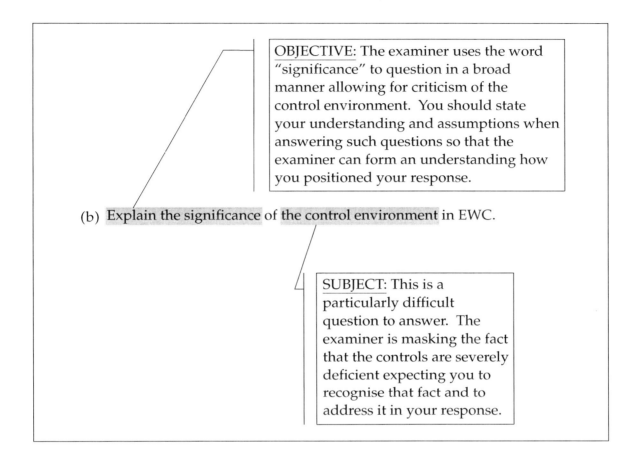

I The corporate governance environment, the policies and procedures, the structure of the organisation and management style all play a part in the quality and effectiveness of management control systems. You are required to synthesis these areas in responding to the issue surrounding the quality (or lack thereof to be more precise) in this case.

D Marks will depend upon the extent to which you synthesise the aspects impinging on the quality of the control environment and how you relate that to the specific case at hand.

(c) From the perspective of a newly appointed non-executive director, evaluate the financial, non-financial quantitative and qualitative controls in EWC in the context of EWC's goals and the risks facing EWC.

A

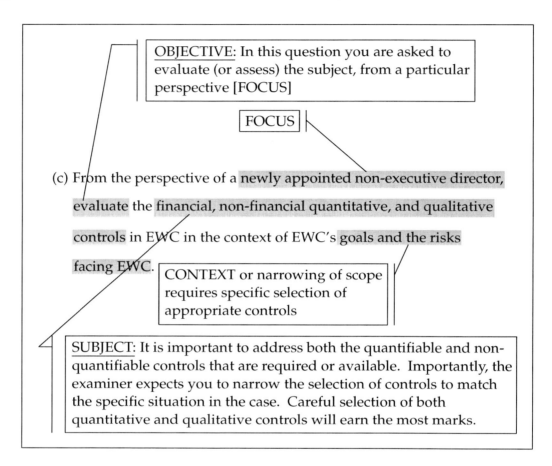

OBJECTIVE: In this question you are asked to evaluate (or assess) the subject, from a particular perspective [FOCUS]

FOCUS

(c) From the perspective of a newly appointed non-executive director, evaluate the financial, non-financial quantitative, and qualitative controls in EWC in the context of EWC's goals and the risks facing EWC.

CONTEXT or narrowing of scope requires specific selection of appropriate controls

SUBJECT: It is important to address both the quantifiable and non-quantifiable controls that are required or available. Importantly, the examiner expects you to narrow the selection of controls to match the specific situation in the case. Careful selection of both quantitative and qualitative controls will earn the most marks.

I One tool that could best guide your response is the Balanced Scorecard. Combined with the corporate governance compliance requirements that dictate non-executive directors' behaviour and responsibilities you will be well equipped to assess or evaluate the [quality or lack thereof] of both the financial and non-financial controls.

D The response should address the financial and non-financial controls in terms of both quantitative and qualitative measures focusing on the requirements for compliance from the perspective of the non-executive directors as opposed to the executive directors who have more active responsibilities and lesser expectations for monitoring and audit as is the requirements directed by the legislation/codes imposing corporate governance compliance.

Examiner's Answer to November 2007 – Question Four

(a)

The major risks facing EWC are reputational, business and reporting.

Reputational risks arise because EWC is overlooking unscrupulous practices in dealing with customers, competitors and suppliers. These will most likely impact on future business as unscrupulous practices are brought to the attention of the press and public. This attention is also likely to affect customer retention and make winning new customers more difficult, and may lead to difficulties in obtaining supply. It may also make it difficult to attract employees to the company, especially ethical ones.

Business risk arises as a consequence of poor reputation. However, business risk may also arise from the single-minded pursuit of growth and low costs. EWC may find that its cost reduction process results in a lack of ability to deliver what it has sold to customers, or that quality declines, customer service is poor or inadequate management leads to poor decision-making. The major business risk is therefore not achieving the sales and profitability targets that have been set, leading to unsatisfactory shareholder returns. The constant price pressure placed on suppliers by EWC could cause the financial failure of those suppliers and lead to an interruption to EWC's supply chain. The attention to supplier profitability is important. A f urther business risk arises from the flat management structure and the potential inability to deal with unexpected events such as business shocks or the resignation of key staff. Given its emphasis on sales growth, EWC also faces the risk of overtrading which could lead to pressure on working capital and inadequate financing.

Reporting risk, that is inaccurate or late financial results, may follow from inadequate administration. There is also the possibility that the approach to growth and profits, together with the rewards associated with that, will lead to the fabrication of financial results, as occurred with Enron, WorldCom and others.

(b)

The control environment is the attitude, awareness and actions of directors and managers in relation to the importance of internal controls, including the organisation's culture and values and the style of management. The control environment is the necessary background for internal control procedures to be developed and operate effectively.

The culture within EWC is one that allows unscrupulous practices and minimises administration. There are likely to be few internal controls given the limited attention to policies and procedures. However, any internal controls that do exist may well be undermined by this culture and the single-minded pursuit of growth and profits to the exclusion it seems, of other factors. The reward and penalty systems in place are likely to support unscrupulous practices and it is likely that over time, the majority of employees will tend to behave in unethical ways.

The control environment in EWC evidenced by the culture that top management subscribes to is therefore likely to accentuate reputational, business and reporting risks.

(c)

A non-executive director (NED) is expected to take an independent, distanced and longer-term responsibility for looking after the interests of shareholders and broader stakeholders. EWC appears to take a very short-term view. Financial controls express financial targets and spending limits. These appear to dominate in EWC. Budget targets are stretching and this may demotivate some employees, whilst encouraging others to engage in any practices that will lead to those results being achieved. Cost reduction is also likely to lead to poor practices. Management accounts should be produced regularly to enable monitoring of financial performance by the Board.

Non-financial quantitative controls comprise targets and measures that support financial goals. The idea of the Balanced Scorecard and similar models is that financial results are lagging indicators of performance. Leading indicators of performance focus on customers, process efficiency and innovation. However, in EWC those non-financial targets that exist are exclusively focused on customers and markets. It seems that in terms of targets and measures, processes are not considered important, nor is innovation, beyond cost reduction. This may result in poor quality, late deliveries, and inefficiency. The scorecard used by EWC is therefore seriously unbalanced.

Qualitative controls comprise the formal and informal structures; the policies and procedures; plans; incentives and personnel controls. In EWC, these controls all support the objective of sales growth and profitability. There is a flat management structure and formal policies and procedures are minimised. The dominant form of qualitative control is the incentive system that encourages the achievement of targets and discourages failure by facilitating those deemed unsuccessful to leave the company (although how this is done is unclear from the scenario).

One positive aspect of the controls that are in place is that they support EWC's goals of sales growth and profitability. Whether these goals are in the medium- or longer-term realistic or achievable is one matter, but the controls do support growth. However, these controls do not take reputational, business and reporting risks into consideration and may in fact accentuate those risks rather than mitigate them.

While it is not necessarily the role of NEDs to monitor all such control data, it is their responsibility to ensure that such controls are in place and are being monitored by the executive directors and managers.

INTERNAL AUDIT

November 2007 – Question Five

Requirement

"Effective internal control, internal audit, audit committee and corporate governance are all inter-related".

Discuss this statement with reference to:

(a) How internal audit should contribute to the effectiveness of internal control?

(7 marks)

(b) How an audit committee should contribute to the effectiveness of internal audit?

(9 marks)

(c) The role of an audit committee in promoting good corporate governance.

(9 marks)
(Total for Question Five = 25 marks)
(Total for Section B = 50 marks)

"Effective internal control, internal audit, audit committee and corporate governance are all inter-related".

Discuss this statement with reference to:

(a) How internal audit should contribute to the effectiveness of internal control.

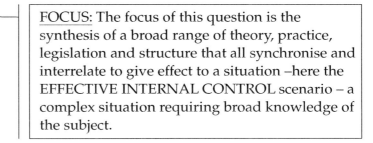

FOCUS: The focus of this question is the synthesis of a broad range of theory, practice, legislation and structure that all synchronise and interrelate to give effect to a situation –here the EFFECTIVE INTERNAL CONTROL scenario – a complex situation requiring broad knowledge of the subject.

"Effective internal control, internal audit, audit committee and corporate governance are all inter-related".

Discuss this statement with reference to:

(a) How internal audit should contribute to the effectiveness of internal control.

OBJECTIVE: The approach here is to discuss internal audit ONLY as it contributes to the effectiveness of internal control. The response should only include those elements that contribute to the control dimension. The tendency here is for respondents to discuss internal audit generally instead of the specific requirement.

SUBJECT: Internal control is the central focus requiring the application of synthesised FOCUS aspects. Note that the focus could have been risk, a specific risk or process within the IM system all of which would have otherwise directed the solution.

I The range of tools here is broad. The internal audit plan with techniques that can support management control, the pick of management controls and risk management all synergise to construct the response.

D Reflecting the integration of risk management, management controls and internal audit, particularly where the process of internal auditing provides support, feedback and transparency to internal control will earn maximum marks.

"Effective internal control, internal audit, audit committee and corporate governance are all inter-related".

Discuss this statement with reference to:

(b) How an audit committee should contribute to the effectiveness of internal audit?

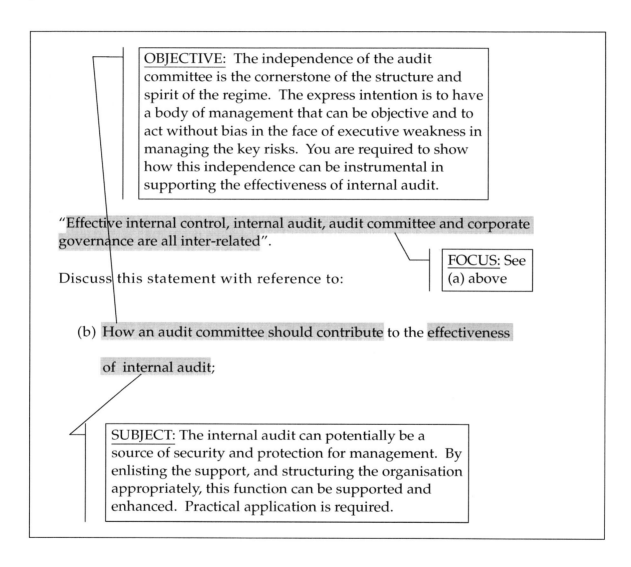

I This response requires practical insight as to how the reporting lines, organisational structuring and the independence of the audit committee can be configured to enhance the effectiveness of the internal audit function.

D The examiner will reward practical and constructive suggestions where the strengths of the independent audit committee can be leveraged to support the internal audit function. The potential shortcomings, loss of objectivity and manipulation potential could provide a critical counter-argument.

"Effective internal control, internal audit, audit committee and corporate governance are all inter-related".

Discuss this statement with reference to:

(c) The role of an audit committee in promoting good corporate governance.

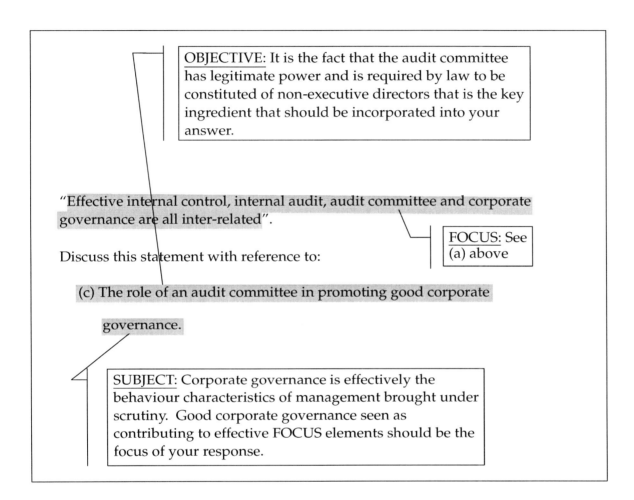

I   The terms of reference, aims and objectives of the Combined Code (or Sarbanes Oxley in the USA) and the Stock Exchange rules serve as the basis for the response to this question.

D   The self-regulating requirement within the board of directors through the medium of the audit committee (amongst other committees) based upon legislative platforms and the vested power to influence the behaviour of senior executives as envisaged by the corporate governance legislative/guidance system forms the cornerstone upon which a good answer would be constructed.

Examiner's Answer to November 2007 – Question Five

(a)

An internal audit contributes to the effectiveness of internal controls by ensuring that internal controls take into account the risks facing the organisation and that risks are reduced to a level acceptable to the board. The focus of risk-based internal auditing is to be able to provide assurances to the audit committee that risk management processes are operating as intended. This is achieved by ensuring that the risk management system has a sound design; that management's responses to risks are adequate and effective in reducing risks to an acceptable level; and that a framework of controls is in place to mitigate risks.

Whilst managers are expected to put in place controls to mitigate risk, they are also expected to deliver financial performance and this may place managers in a conflict of interest. This may lead them to minimise controls where they see these as unnecessary, costly or restrictive. As a result of this potential conflict, the internal audit function has an important role to play in ensuring that controls are in place.

Although it is management's responsibility to identify and manage risks, to effectively assess the adequacy of internal controls, internal auditors need to have expertise in risk management: how risks are identified, assessed and managed. The risk management system will itself need to be audited in order to ensure that it can be relied upon. Internal audit matches its audit programme with the degree of risk maturity in the organisation. Risk management will inform the priorities for the internal audit plan. In particular, internal audit should identify high risk matters and control deficiencies so that actions can be taken to improve those controls and so avoid, reduce or mitigate risks.

(b)

The primary responsibility for providing assurance on the adequacy of controls and risk management lies with management. However, audit committees require independent and objective assurance to validate the assurances they are receiving from management.

Internal audit is an independent and objective function which may be a department of an organisation or an outsourced function which examines and evaluates risk management, internal control and governance processes. The core role of internal audit is to provide assurance that the main business risks are being managed and that internal controls are operating effectively. Internal audit should have a charter which describes its purpose, authority and responsibility, which should be reviewed annually.

The Head of Internal Audit should be appointed by and report to the audit committee and be independent of the chief financial officer (CFO), although the Head will have to work closely with the CFO. The Head should develop an internal audit plan based on risk assessments, submit internal audit plans to the audit committee for approval, implement the approved plan, and maintain a team with knowledge and capacity to carry out the plan.

An audit committee contributes to the effectiveness of the internal audit function by ensuring that:

- the internal audit charter is adequate,
- the Head of Internal Audit is independent and objective,
- there are adequate internal audit resources to provide the necessary support for management assurances and enable the audit committee to advise the board so that the board can give its report to shareholders.

The audit committee must also approve internal audit plans and exercise its own expertise and judgement that risks have been properly assessed and that internal audit plans address the most significant risks. The audit committee must also carefully consider internal audit reports and ensure that the organisation implements recommendations that have the audit committee's support. Finally, the audit committee should monitor and review the effectiveness of internal audit and may seek the opinion of external auditors in making that assessment.

(c)

Corporate governance has increased in importance on the corporate agenda as a result of the Combined Code (in the UK), Sarbanes-Oxley (in the US) and similar reforms throughout the world, as a response to major corporate collapses of Enron and WorldCom (in the US) and many other large companies in many countries. Institutional investors have also promoted improved governance processes as part of the move to encourage sustainability of earnings.

Corporate overnance is the method by which companies are directed and controlled through Boards of Directors which establish corporate aims, provide leadership, supervise management and report to shareholders. The Board's role is to provide entrepreneurial leadership within a framework of controls that enable risk to be managed.

The Combined Code recommends that Boards appoint an audit committee of independent non-executive directors to assist the board in fulfilling its stewardship function by reviewing systems of internal control, the external audit process, the work of internal auditors and external auditors and financial reporting to shareholders. The Board will appoint and remunerate non-executive directors, some of whom will be appointed to the audit committee. The role of appointing and remunerating board members is normally a function of a Nominations or Remuneration Committee of the Board.

The main roles of the audit committee are:

*   monitoring the integrity of financial statements;
*   internal control and risk management systems;
*   monitoring and reviewing the effectiveness of internal audit;
*   appointing, monitoring and reviewing the effectiveness of external audit.

Importantly, the audit committee is a committee of the Board and should have its own terms of reference. Although the Board delegates its authority to the audit committee, it retains its responsibility. The audit committee reports to the Board and makes recommendations appropriate to its responsibilities. It is the Board's responsibility to review the effectiveness of internal control (and not just financial control) on a continuous basis. The Board makes an annual assessment of internal control which forms part of the Board's reporting to shareholders. In this assessment the Board must acknowledge that it is responsible for the internal control system and for reviewing its effectiveness. In making this assessment, the audit committee and Board will rely to some extent on the reports from the company's external auditors. In the US, Sarbanes-Oxley has a particular emphasis on internal control over financial reporting and does not give the same prominence to the role of the audit committee as does the Combined Code. For companies listed in the US, external auditors report on management's assessment, but this is not a feature of UK legislation. The Board should review the audit committee's effectiveness annually.

By monitoring risk management and internal controls, the audit committee and the Board itself contribute to good corporate governance, the benefits of which can include: reduced risk, improved performance, improved access to capital markets, stakeholder confidence, and demonstrated transparency and accountability.

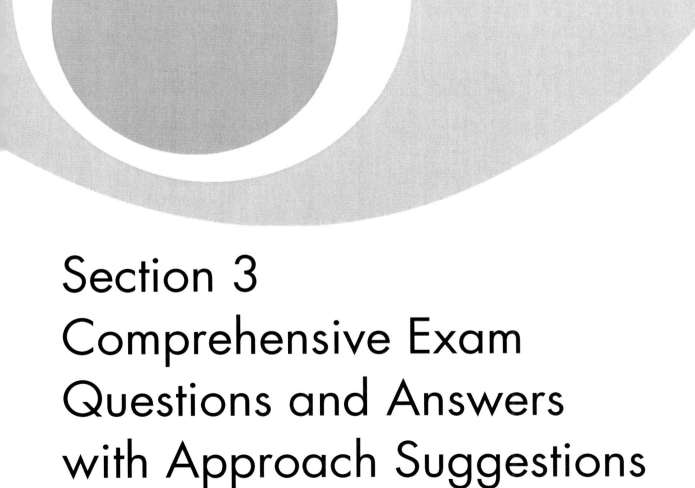

Section 3
Comprehensive Exam
Questions and Answers
with Approach Suggestions

Comprehensive Exam Questions and Answers with Approach Suggestions

Approach suggestions

When attempting any detailed case study the recommendation remains that you approach the case by reading at the "required" first. This is a critical first step to ensure that you do not form an opinion of what you expect the questions to be. All too often, participants read the case and then form an opinion of what they expect the question to be which blinds them to the specific requirements set by the examiner. The recommended *R.A.I.D.©* method assists in preventing this preconceived perception of the examiners requirements and goes on to provide a mechanism for analysing the question in terms of its component parts.

The analysis section ensures that the subject of the question is identified and clearly distinguished from the objective(s). In so doing, the participant determines "what is to be acted upon" (subject) and how the subject is to be acted upon (objective(s)).

In applied questions of the nature in this module, the examiner is often looking for two key components. The first of these is knowledge and recall of the theory and content of the CIMA *Learning System*. The second component is a demonstration by the participant that they are able to apply the theory in practice. In general, though marks weighting is on the application requirement. However, if the respondent is not able to recall the theory and content then, application is not possible at all.

Memorising and recall

 In modules of this nature, the participant is expected to memorise large volumes of theory and information. During the study process, the use of mind mapping techniques developed by Tony Buzan or a similar summarizing and recall aid is highly recommended. (See Buzan, T. & B., *The Mind Map Book (Fully Illustrated Edition)*, ISBN: 1406612790).

May 2007 Exam – Question One

 Examiners' recommendation: The indicative time for answering this section is 90 minutes.

ACB is a stock exchange listed company that designs and assembles small passenger aircraft which it sells to regional airlines throughout the world. ACB is highly regarded by its airline customers for the quality of its aircraft. ACB is also recognised for meeting contractual commitments through on-time delivery. The company generates profits before interest and taxes of about 5% of sales. However, due to the depressed nature of the airline industry and competition from foreign manufacturers, the company has modest growth targets. About 60 aircraft are delivered each year.

Competitive Advantage

The company's competitive advantage is its ability to take a standard aircraft design and customise it to the varying needs of its customers. This includes, for example, changes in engine size, passenger capacity, configuration, and electronic equipment. The cycle time from signed order to delivery is about 18 months.

Pricing and Sales Terms

ACB sets the price of its completed aircraft in the customer's currency. The fixed price is converted to ACB's home currency using exchange rates applicable at the time contracts are signed. Progress payments are made on order and throughout the production process, but the balance of approximately 60% of the selling price of the aircraft is made on delivery to the airline. Any delivery delays are classed as a breach of ACB's contract for which it incurs significant financial penalties.

Production and Supply Chain

The manufacture of all the aircraft components has been subcontracted to about 200 suppliers located across several continents. The cost of purchased components constitutes 70% of the final aircraft selling price. Suppliers are selected on the basis of quality, reliability and cost. Contracts with each supplier include prices established in the supplier's currency and incorporate price increases and anticipated efficiency savings over the next two years. This enables accurate forecasting of material costs by ACB. As each component is produced to satisfy the differing requirements of each aircraft, any delay in receipt of any component will delay final assembly. A distribution company has the contract to transport all components to ACB's factory and a combination of bar-coding and satellite tracking technology enables the precise location of all components to be tracked from despatch through to receipt by ACB.

There are five major production operations at ACB's factory: four relate to component assembly and one to final assembly. The four component assembly operations are fuselage, wings, engines, and electronics. All four component assemblies are brought together in a large hangar where the final aircraft assembly takes place. ACB operates its factory on a just-in-time (JIT) basis to minimise inventory. Production scheduling for each of the four component assembly operations must be integrated so that the final assembly can take place on schedule.

IT Support

ACB uses a sophisticated enterprise resource planning system (ERPS) to manage its supply chain, purchase ordering, production scheduling, accounting and performance management, and customer relationship management. The company also relies on an electronic data interchange (EDI) system to track component purchase orders from their despatch by suppliers to receipt at ACB's factory.

Quality Control

Aircraft manufacture is highly regulated with stringent quality control and safety requirements. ACB has always maintained the highest standards. The government's Aircraft Inspection Agency makes regular inspections of component and final assembly quality in order to ensure annual re-licensing of ACB as an aircraft manufacturer.

Costing and Pricing

The cost of each aircraft is estimated from a bill of materials for components and a labour routing, both of which take into account the customisation of each aircraft. Price negotiations follow the cost estimation process and discounts are given for quantity and the significance of the customer to ACB in terms of past and anticipated sales.

Overhead costs are traced to products through an activity-based costing system, based on cost drivers established for eight significant business processes. Profits are calculated for each aircraft and each order (which may be for several aircraft) and customer profitability analysis is used to support future sales efforts.

Risk Management and Governance

The company has a Risk Management Group at senior management level that maintains a register of major risks, carries out risk assessments in terms of their likelihood and consequences, identifies appropriate risk responses, and reports to each meeting of the Audit Committee. IT risks and foreign currency exposures require highly specialised attention and responsibility for these risks is delegated to the IT Department and Treasury Department respectively.

The ERPS and EDI systems are managed by the in-house IT department which has long-serving and highly skilled staff who have developed comprehensive operating procedures and business continuity plans. ACB's Treasury department primarily uses matching techniques to offset foreign exchange exposures in each currency but does use forward contracts where exposures in some currencies are deemed unacceptable.

The Board of Directors emphasises strategy and monitors sales and delivery performance. It aims to ensure that sales are spread evenly over different regions so as not to be disproportionately affected by political or economic changes. The general approach to risk management is to have a portfolio of customers, products and suppliers, so as to minimise sensitivity to any one factor that might jeopardise the company's success. The Board reviews assessments made by the Aircraft Inspection Agency and is actively involved in rectifying any problems identified.

The company's Audit Committee, composed of independent directors, monitors the risk assessments made by managers, ensures that internal controls are adequate and approves the company's internal audit plan each year. The Audit Committee also monitors all monthly financial performance information while the internal audit function spends a considerable proportion of its resources ensuring that financial performance information produced by the ERPS is accurate for management decision-making and financial reporting purposes.

Requirements

(a) State the recommended components of any organisation's risk management strategy and evaluate ACB's approach to risk management in terms of those components.

(12 marks)

(b) Identify the major categories of risk facing ACB and evaluate the controls adopted by ACB in relation to each category.

(28 marks)

(c) Risk treatment (or risk response) is an important component of risk management strategy. Explain what is meant by risk treatment and its benefits to a Board of Directors.

(10 marks)

(Total for Question One = 50 marks)

(Total for Section A = 50 marks)

(a) State the recommended components of any organisation's risk management strategy and evaluate ACB's approach to risk management in terms of those components.

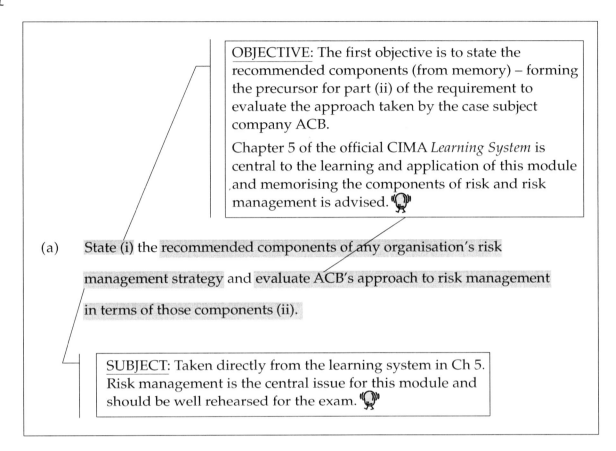

I Recall of theory from the official CIMA *Learning System*. The focus is on chapters 3, 5, 6 and 7 with aspects of risk from chapter 13 and 14. Recall of risk categorisation, associated controls and internal audit procedure are central to handling the question.

D It is clear from the examiners' suggested solution that the weighting in this question is towards detailed application of the theory. It is important to address the range of risks and their management strategies and then relate them to case specifics.

(b) Identify the major categories of risk facing ACB and evaluate the controls adopted by ACB in relation to each category.

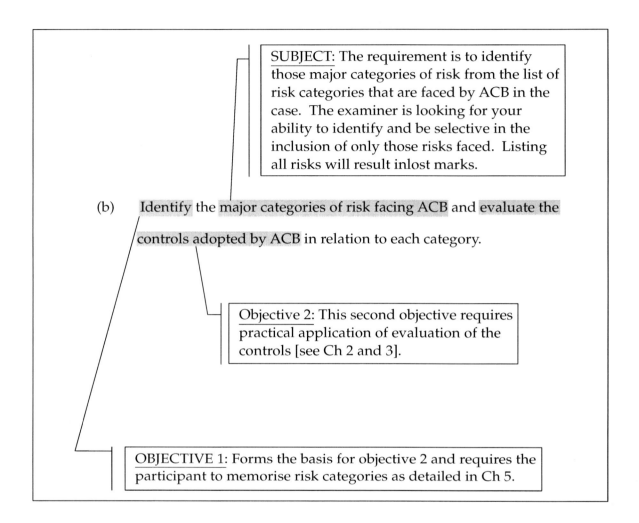

SUBJECT: The requirement is to identify those major categories of risk from the list of risk categories that are faced by ACB in the case. The examiner is looking for your ability to identify and be selective in the inclusion of only those risks faced. Listing all risks will result inlost marks.

(b) Identify the major categories of risk facing ACB and evaluate the controls adopted by ACB in relation to each category.

Objective 2: This second objective requires practical application of evaluation of the controls [see Ch 2 and 3].

OBJECTIVE 1: Forms the basis for objective 2 and requires the participant to memorise risk categories as detailed in Ch 5.

I The selection of primary risks and associated secondly systems risks from the official CIMA *Learning System* [Ch 5, 8 and 9].

D The Examiner is testing your ability to synthesise the risks and their controls across business operations and IT systems. Your ability to demonstrate the interactive nature of controls upon a specific range of business and systems risks, associated with this specific case, generates maximum marks.

(c) Risk treatment (or risk response) is an important component of risk management strategy. Explain what is meant by risk treatment and its benefits to a Board of Directors.

 With the current flash of banking failures and an expected rise in corporate default participants could legitimately expect this type of question to become more significant in future exams.

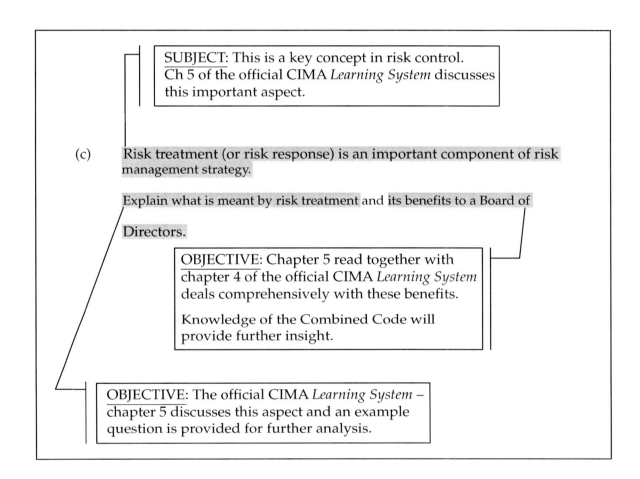

I Risk treatments dealt with in the official CIMA *Learning System* chapter 5 with insights into the requirements for the directors of listed companies dealt with in chapter 4. Participants should also consult the Combined Code.

The Examiner linked internal audit to this process and participants are recommended to synthesise control and management issues wherever applicable as is the case with this question.

D The explanation of risk treatments forms the backdrop for the participant to demonstrate practical capability in assisting appropriate risk treatments, management, insurance, etc. Practical application forms the basis for marks maximisation.

Examiners' Answers

The answers that follow are fuller and more comprehensive than would have been expected from a well-prepared candidate. They have been written in this way to aid teaching, study and revision for tutors and candidates alike.

May 2007 Exam – Examiners' Answers to Question One

(a)

All organisations should develop a risk management strategy, which will include:

- the risk appetite of the organisation, that is, the level of risk it finds acceptable;
- the risk assessment and evaluation processes the organisation practises;
- its preferred options for risk treatment (for example, retention, avoidance, reduction, transfer);
- who is responsible in the organisation for risk management; and
- how reporting and monitoring processes take place.

There is no evidence of individuals or a group being charged with actively identifying risks. It is insufficient to simply react to risks that become generally apparent.

There is no evidence of an explicit determination of ACB's risk appetite which would provide a consistent reference point. The method of risk treatment adopted seems to rely on a portfolio approach. However, there is potential for significant risks to eventuate due to the company's exposure to its supply chain, information technology and foreign exchange.

The company's Risk Management Group does carry out risk assessments, treatment and reporting. However, it is not clear from the scenario whether internal controls are related to risk or whether more traditional methods of internal control are in use.

IT risks appear to be managed by the IT department and foreign exchange risks by the Treasury department but there appears to be little oversight of these risks by the Risk Management Group or the Audit Committee.

There is an internal audit process but, again, it is unclear the extent to which this is linked to risk assessment as the main emphasis seems to be on financial controls. Consequently, it seems likely that improvements could be made in internal controls, internal audit and reporting processes to support the established risk management function.

The risk management process is managed by the Audit Committee of ACB. While governance does appear to incorporate risk management, internal controls and internal audit, it may be that the Audit Committee is overly reliant on financial rather than non-financial information.

(b)
Supply chain risk
A major risk faced by ACB is a failure of its supply chain which would stop aircraft production and result in significant penalties from airlines where delivery dates are not met. Although the Board does seem to monitor ACB's delivery performance, any potential failure of suppliers or the logistics company constitutes a significant risk. There is no evidence

that there is dual sourcing of either component or logistics suppliers or of any contingency back-up capacity for transport or production line operations.

Reputation risk

Failure of ACB's supply chain will cause delays in delivery which will not only incur financial penalties but future orders may be lost resulting in a loss of reputation and lower profits in the future.

The stringent quality and safety requirements are being maintained but any reduction in standards due to either supplier failure in component manufacture or assembly problems would result in a loss of ACB's licence and consequently its ability to trade. Although there is active involvement by the Board in rectifying problems once they have been identified by the Inspection Agency, little is known of any internal controls for maintaining quality and safety standards. Any serious problems will also result in a significant effect on ACB's reputation.

Economic and political risk

There are economic and political risks resulting from trade with different countries over long time periods, although the Board's adoption of a portfolio approach may be effective in offsetting risks. It is evident that the market in which ACB sells is depressed and there is significant competition, but apart from conservative growth estimates, ACB appears to have no risk management strategy to cope with potentially declining performance over time.

There are also industry-specific risks. Even if ACB maintains its market share, terrorism, fuel costs or restrictive regulations and taxes could result in industry stagnation. Consideration may therefore be given to whether some form of diversification might be appropriate and/or research and development activity into reducing the environmental impact of the aircraft produced.

IT risk

Allied to the supply chain risk is the risk of failure of the IT systems on which ACB is so dependent. Enterprise resource planning systems (ERPS) take a whole of business approach and capture accounting, operational, customer and supplier data in data warehouses from which management reports are produced. ERPS is the central method by which companies manage their supply chain, customer relationship management, activity-based costing and performance measurement. It is assumed that ACB's ERPS carries out these functions. Consequently, ACB is highly reliant on data accuracy and information security to support its operations.

While operating procedures and continuity plans appear to be in existence, it is unclear whether or not these have been tested. There is a dependence on highly skilled IT staff who may leave ACB's employment.

Even though responsibility is delegated to the IT Department, there still needs to be some form of accountability to the Audit Committee by specialists from IT who are able to report, in plain language, on IT matters.

Exchange rate fluctuations

A major risk is from exchange rate fluctuations for purchased components, which are paid for in the currency of each supplier's country. Offsetting or exacerbating this risk is that of exchange rate fluctuations for the supply of completed aircraft, as a result of exchange rate changes between the date on which contracts are signed and when progress payments or final deliveries are made. Internal hedging could take place by invoicing in ACB's home currency. External hedging techniques such as forward exchange contracts could be used to provide more extensive risk management of this exposure.

Even though responsibility is delegated to the Treasury Department, there still needs to be some form of accountability to the Audit Committee by specialists from Treasury who are able to report, in plain language, on currency risk exposure.

Cost control

A further risk relates to cost control. Bills of materials and labour routings exist, and provided these are kept up-to-date, cost estimates should be accurate. However, customisation results in variable costs per aircraft. These are estimated at the time prices are negotiated. Cost increases need to be taken into account, especially as the cycle time is so long. This appears to be covered in supplier agreements but there is a risk of labour and overhead cost increases (comprising 25% of the selling price). While backflushing eliminates routine accounting tasks, it will not necessarily identify cost overruns in labour or components between standard and actual costs. Overhead cost control is necessary, even under an activity-based costing system. Product and customer profitability analysis will assist in identifying problems, but these will only be after the event.

Other risks may be identified that are generally applicable to businesses, such as personnel risks relating to senior management recruitment and retention, fraud, asset loss, etc.

(c)

Risk treatment (also called risk response) is the process of selecting and implementing measures to modify risk that has been identified. This may include risk control/mitigation, risk avoidance, risk transfer, risk financing (for example, insurance), etc.

Risk response involves determining and documenting:

- A policy of defining the organisation's attitude to a particular risk and the objectives of the risk response.
- Individual accountability for the management of the risk, with a nominated person having the expertise and authority to effectively manage the risk.
- The management processes currently used to manage the risk.
- Recommended business processes to reduce the residual risk to an acceptable level.
- Key performance measures to enable management to assess and monitor risk.
- Independent expertise to assess the adequacy of the risk response.
- Contingency plans to manage or mitigate a major loss following the occurrence of an event.

Risk treatment (or response) enables the Board to see easily which risks have been addressed and those where risk management procedures remain outstanding, and in both cases which individuals are responsible. This permits management by exception. It will enable a Board of Directors to better understand and react to:

- The nature and extent of risks facing the organisation.
- The extent and categories of risk which it regards as acceptable for the organisation to bear (the risk strategy).
- The likelihood of risks materialising.
- The costs and benefits of risk responses.

Consideration of these factors enables the Board to have evidence that it has carried out its responsibilities for risk management.

Risk treatment (or response) may be:

- *Avoidance:* action is taken to exit the activities giving rise to risk, such as a product line or a geographical market, or a whole business unit. These are high risk events.
- *Reduction:* action is taken to mitigate (i.e. reduce) the risk likelihood or impact, or both, generally via internal controls. These risks occur more frequently but have less impact.
- *Sharing:* Action is taken to transfer a portion of the risk through, for example, insurance, pooling risks, hedging or outsourcing. These are significant risks, which occur rarely.
- *Acceptance:* no action is taken to affect likelihood or impact. These have low impact even when they do occur, which may be frequent.

Each response needs to be considered in terms of its effect on reducing the likelihood and/or impact of the risk. A comparison of gross and net risk enables a review of risk response effectiveness and possible alternative management options.

- *Gross risk* involves the assessment of risk before the application of any controls, transfer or management responses.
- *Net risk* involves the assessment of risk, taking into account the application of any controls, transfer or management response to the risk under consideration.

Nov 2007 Exam – Question One

The NOP Group is one of the world's largest clothing retailers and had a turnover in excess of £2,000 million for the year ended 30 September 2007. The group's clothes are sold in Europe, East Asia, North America and Australia and New Zealand. The clothes are made for NOP by a number of approved contractors in China, Sri Lanka, Thailand and India. The clothes are designed by employees of NOP at the company's headquarters in London, England. The designers base their ideas on what has attracted them when they have attended the previews of the latest styles at the fashion shows presented by the world's leading fashion houses. NOP operates to a four month lead time which runs from the start of the design process through to the first appearance of the new styles in the retail stores.

NOP's clothes are targeted at the mid to high priced sector of the market and are sold under several brand names. NOP tries to match brands to differing customer profiles, and in doing so recognises that its customers' ages are an important factor. Within the 18–25 year customer age group, brands are 'uni-sex'.

NOP operates across four geographic business units, with each managed as a profit centre. The group has differing arrangements for its retail outlets across the world, as shown below:

Business Unit	Outlet Arrangement
Europe (UK, France, Italy)	Group owned shops
USA and Canada	Franchise agreements
Asia (Japan, Thailand, China, Singapore)	Joint ventures with department stores
Australia and New Zealand	Joint venture with a distributor

The Group is a signatory to an ethical code of conduct (see extracts in the additional information below) which has been developed for use within the clothing sector, and it produces a separate social and environmental report which it views as complementary to its annual report. As part of its environmental protection policy, NOP has also declared a commitment not to send waste to landfill sites from 2008 onwards and will make arrangements for all company waste to be recycled.

The Group's Treasurer regards NOP as highly exposed to currency risk, and therefore requires that all open positions with an equivalent value in excess of £100,000 are hedged. Responsibility for hedging arrangements lies with the Finance Director of each of NOP's four regional business units. Capital gearing is kept at a low level compared to NOP's competitors, and the market value of debt equalled just 30% of the market value of equity at the balance sheet date of 30th September 2007. The Group Directors' remuneration, as detailed in Note 3 below, is linked to medium-term financial targets.

The Group's shares are listed on both the London and the New York stock exchanges. NOP's share price has fallen by 15% over the last six weeks, compared with an average fall of 10% for the general retail sector, and 8% for fashion retailers. A meeting of the Board of Directors has been called to address the problem.

The Group Finance Director thinks that a share price recovery could be stimulated by a well targeted cost cutting exercise. The production and transportation costs being charged by suppliers are considered too high, as they amount to 75% of the cost of goods sold. Initial estimates suggest that there is scope to reduce each of these costs by around 5%. Profit is further eroded by high employee costs, especially in Europe, where they equal 18%

of sales, compared to an industry average of 12%. The Group Finance Director believes that increasing the proportion of part-time sales staff could bring employee costs in line with the industry average.

The Group Marketing Director proposes an alternative solution, as he believes that a new advertising campaign would stop the decline in the share price. The campaign would focus on the group's most glamorous product ranges and would use international film stars to promote the clothes. The average gross margin on all clothes sales across the group varies significantly. For some products in the UK and Japan it is 45%, but it is as low as 6% for some products in Thailand and Singapore. The glamour ranges earn an average gross margin of 22% and sales of these ranges account for 15% of group revenue, but it is thought that the advertising campaign could significantly boost global sales of these high mark-up products with no accompanying sales loss elsewhere.

Additional Information

1. Extracts from key financial statistics for the preceding two years:

	2005 £million	2006 £million
Sales*	2,400	3,120
Gross Profit (excluding joint ventures)	480	625
Distribution costs	72	50
Profit/loss from joint ventures	(350)	180
Net Interest payable	24	22
Dividend yield on year end share price	1·5%	1·5%
UK Share Price (year end)	465 pence	490 pence
Price index for UK retail shares (Base 100 in 1997)	680	782

The current (November 2007) share price is 480 pence

*Sales are split across the regions as follows: Europe 60%; USA & Canada 20%; Asia 12%; Australia and New Zealand 8%.

2. The Ethical Code of Conduct covers conditions and terms of employment within NOP and in NOP's suppliers, and includes the following requirements:

- Payment of the legal minimum level of wages (or industry average) whichever is higher.
- No use of forced labour, and freedom for employees to join a trade union and/or engage in collective bargaining.
- Safe and hygienic working conditions.
- A commitment not to use child labour, that is, aged below 15.
- Working hours kept to normal national levels or local industry standards.

Remuneration of Group Executive Directors

3. In addition to a fixed, market based salary, plus pension and health scheme benefits, group directors are entitled to performance related pay. The performance related pay usually represents over 50% of each director's annual remuneration and is based upon the following terms:
- A variable bonus is payable if performance meets or exceeds pre-determined annual targets for NOP's profit before tax. Achieving target performance earns the directors a

bonus of 55% of their annual salary, and this rises to a maximum of 150% for performance more than 20% above the target level.

- Half of the variable bonus is granted in cash, and the rest is paid in shares, which must be held for a minimum of three years.

4. Remuneration of business unit directors and other senior managers

In common with the executive directors, other senior managers in NOP are paid partly on the basis of performance. Senior staff can earn bonuses paid in shares, which carry no minimum holding period requirement. The bonus rates are dependent upon performance relative to earnings per share growth targets set by the Board of Directors and in recent years have ranged between 50% and 220% of annual salary.

Requirements

(a) Discuss the extent to which **each** of the following characteristics of NOP creates potential risks for the company's shareholders:
- (i)   Branding and marketing strategy
- (ii) Design and procurement strategy
- (iii) Remuneration of senior management and executive directors
- (iv) Corporate Treasury function
- (v)   Social and environmental policies

(30 marks)

(b) Prepare a report to be presented at the board meeting that:

- Explains why the principle of risk ownership at board of director level is a vital form of control, especially in extremely large companies such as NOP.

(5 marks)

- Discusses the relative merits of the Finance Director's and the Marketing Director's proposals. (Your discussion should be from a risk management perspective, and should therefore focus on the risks created by the share price fall and the impact of each proposal on the group's overall risk profile.)

(15 marks)

(Total for Question One = 50 marks)

(Total for Section A = 50 marks)

(a) Discuss the extent to which **each** of the following characteristics of NOP creates potential risks for the company's shareholders:

(i)   Branding and marketing strategy
(ii) Design and procurement strategy
(iii) Remuneration of senior management and executive directors
(iv) Corporate Treasury function
(v)   Social and environmental policies

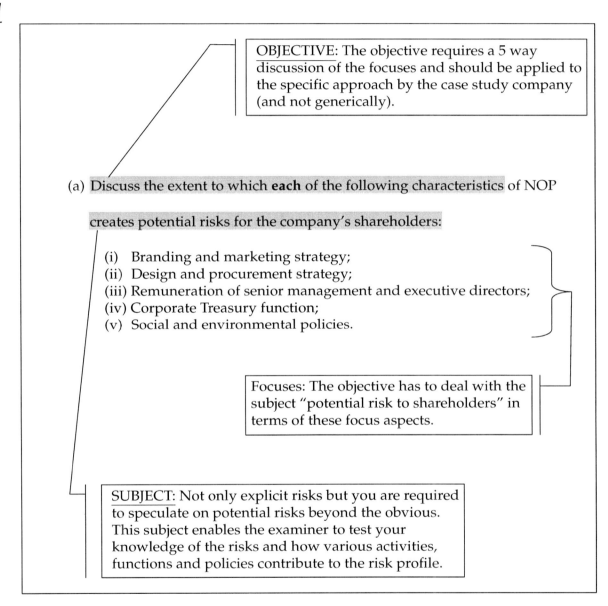

I This comprehensive question draws on your learning across the module content but with a focus on chapter 5. Practical application is central but applying the risk categorisation, corporate governance and policy application with specific reference to corporate social responsibility are essential.

D The examiners have provided a broader that required set of possible responses to this question. While a broad range of possible responses are acceptable to the examiners, you are reminded to keep to time limits and to present relevant application-oriented responses.

$\mathcal{R}$ (b) Prepare a report to be presented at the board meeting that:

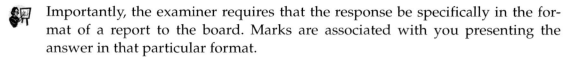

> Importantly, the examiner requires that the response be specifically in the format of a report to the board. Marks are associated with you presenting the answer in that particular format.

- Explains why the principle of risk ownership at board of director level is a vital form of control, especially in extremely large companies such as NOP.

$\mathcal{A}$

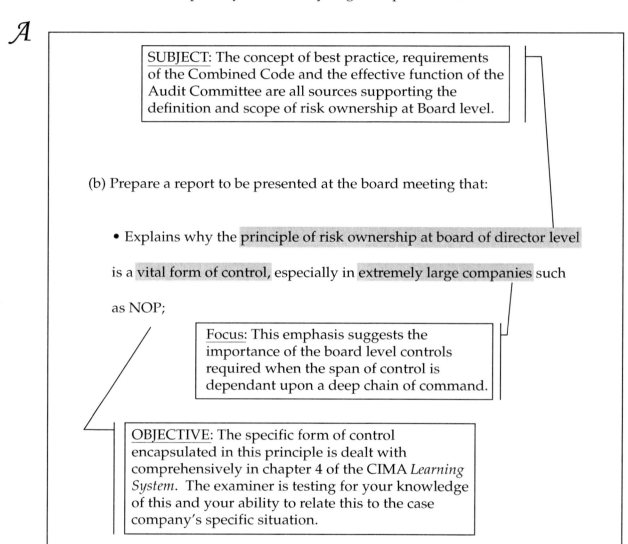

SUBJECT: The concept of best practice, requirements of the Combined Code and the effective function of the Audit Committee are all sources supporting the definition and scope of risk ownership at Board level.

(b) Prepare a report to be presented at the board meeting that:

- Explains why the principle of risk ownership at board of director level is a vital form of control, especially in extremely large companies such as NOP;

Focus: This emphasis suggests the importance of the board level controls required when the span of control is dependant upon a deep chain of command.

OBJECTIVE: The specific form of control encapsulated in this principle is dealt with comprehensively in chapter 4 of the CIMA *Learning System*. The examiner is testing for your knowledge of this and your ability to relate this to the case company's specific situation.

$\mathcal{I}$ In addition to the discussion in Ch 4, knowledge of corporate governance charters is very important. It is important to note the substantial differences of departure between the USA's Sarbanes-Oxley legislation, the UK's Combined Code and the substantially different stakeholder based King II report governing corporate governance in South Africa.

$\mathcal{D}$ The approach demonstrated by the examiners is to take an applied approach to the specific case and reference to specific corporate governance best practice is advised.

(b) Prepare a report to be presented at the board meeting that (also):

- Discusses the relative merits of the Finance Director's and the Marketing Director's proposals. (Your discussion should be from a risk management perspective, and should therefore focus on the risks created by the share price fall and the impact of each proposal on the group's overall risk profile.)

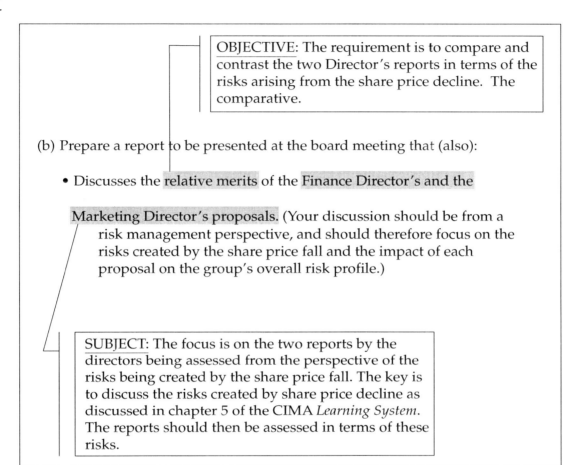

 Gross margin and profit calculations are essential to set the basis for each of the reports to demonstrate the possible cost savings or increment from an increase in sales from advertising increases. These quantitative estimates have to be assessed in terms of the qualitative issues such as the reliability of the projected sales increments from increased advertising (which can be supported by advanced marketing surveys conducted by professional marketing analysis experts at additional cost – not discussed in the case) and the impact of productivity and performance following the proposed cost-cutting recommendations.

D You should calculate the profit impacts forecast by each of the suggestions and then set out the risks associated therewith. What will earn marks, as is supported by the examiners' solutions, is the recommendation of alternative solutions that will counter the more onerous risks anticipated from each of the reports. The examiners have provided a comprehensive solution guide to the question.

Nov 2007 Exam – Examiners' Answer to Question One

(a) (i)

Branding is used by a company as a means of differentiating its products(s) from the competition. A well established and reputable brand name can enable a company to charge higher prices for products that, apart from the branding, appear identical to those of competitors. Branding can therefore be used to raise product profitability.

The information given in the question indicates that NOP uses a variety of brand names, each targeted at a different market segment. It is not, however, clear whether these brands are recognisably linked to the same company, and this may create some risks for NOP. By choosing to use a variety of brand names, there is a risk that NOP has no single image in the minds of consumers. Consequently, there is a risk that brand loyalty will be difficult to maintain as customers get older. For example, if the buyers of the unisex brand targeted at the 18–25 years age group do not know and recognise that a different brand name, aimed at the 30 plus age group is also owned by NOP, then their custom may be lost. There is a risk in not having NOP itself as a brand, and by carrying a wide number of different brands the company may actually find it is effectively at risk of competing against itself.

In addition, there is a risk that the significance of the brand name may vary across the different age groups; teenagers may place a high importance on the brand, but middle aged customers may not. For the customer groups that attach a high significance to the brand name, the company faces a further risk of counterfeiting in certain areas of the world. Counterfeit goods are a constant threat to manufacturers who market their products in South America, Eastern Europe and certain parts of South East Asia, which are all markets in which NOP operates.

NOP is targeting the mid to high price end of the fashion market and in so doing it may be challenging the markets of existing well established so called "designer" labels. There is a risk in following this strategy because the reputation of these brand names is already well established and if product quality does not better the existing labels, then it will be very difficult for NOP to expand its customer base. There is potentially less risk for shareholders in targeting the middle market where brands have some relevance but are not the primary factor that attracts customers.

In terms of marketing, it is clear that NOP uses a range of different routes to market, depending upon the geographical location. The variety of arrangements will increase shareholder risks by making control difficult. Product presentation may vary according to whether the product is being sold in a company owned outlet or one operated under either a franchise or joint venture agreement. Such a lack of consistency poses a challenge to the effective establishment of a global brand. One example of an area where control may be difficult to exercise is that of pricing. The variety of outlet arrangements also adds to the complexity of the warehousing and distribution arrangements.

Examiners' Comment:

The answers that follow are fuller and more comprehensive than would have been expected from a well-prepared candidate. They have been written in this way to aid teaching, study and revision for tutors and candidates alike.

(ii)

Marketing within NOP is global in its reach but all of the design work is centred in London. This approach is presumably adopted to make use of local expertise, but it may also result in clothing designs that are suited to Western rather than global tastes. Sizing may also be a problem, because sizing systems vary around the world and also the average clothes size also differs. Consequently, clothes that are designed to look good on a Western European frame may be much too large and badly shaped for the Japanese or Singaporean markets. Certain types of products may be suited to global consistency of design, but there is a risk for the shareholders of NOP that its fashion clothing may well not fit this business model.

The clothes sold by NOP are supplied by contractors in a range of different countries, and this mixed geography creates currency risks for NOP, which may create a risk to income for shareholders. There are also risks arising from the difficulties of quality control in production locations that are remote from the design location. High levels of quality control are essential to the maintenance of brand image which appears to be the primary source of competitive advantage for NOP. The whole management of the supply chain is relatively complex in NOP because the products are manufactured in four countries in Asia, but need to be distributed to markets scattered across Asia, South America, the Pacific and Europe. In other words the procurement arrangements create risks for investors due to their complexity.

An additional area of possible risk is the need to comply with the ethical code to which NOP is a signatory. Monitoring and auditing suppliers to ensure that they comply with the code requirements is essential if NOP is to avoid the risk of a threat to its reputation. Such monitoring will, however, be costly, and so will create a risk that shareholders will see profits reduced as a consequence.

(iii)

The pay for executive directors in NOP is very dependent upon the level of profit before tax. Shareholders may face a risk that there is no clear definition of the term "profit before tax" and so it is subject to manipulation and change. Furthermore, the bonuses are dependent upon achieving above target for profit before tax, but there is no indication of how these targets are set. Shareholders face the risk that the targets are set by the directors themselves and are therefore relatively easy to achieve. Greater clarity of how the process works is necessary in order to protect the interests of shareholders. Risks are reduced, however, by the mechanism that ensures that only half of the bonus is payable in cash, with the balance in shares. Nonetheless, because the shares only have to be held for three years, the overall remuneration package will encourage short termist thinking amongst the directors and this may not be in the long terms interest of shareholders.

The remuneration method for senior managers is not based upon the same terms as that for the executive directors, and this adds to shareholder risk because there is potential for a conflict of interest between the two parties. The growth rate of earnings per share (EPS) need not be directly correlated with the profit targets that are set for the executives. It could also be argued that setting the bonus levels of 50%–220% of annual salary serve to make the performance bonus the key consideration for senior management. All of their efforts will be focused on achieving the maximum possible bonus, and there is no guarantee that the target rates of EPS growth that are used to determine the bonuses are necessarily in the best interests of shareholders. The targets may be easily attainable, and below the levels being achieved by NOP's main competitors.

The remuneration packages for executives and also for senior managers are heavily dependent upon profit performance, and this creates a cash flow risk for the business because the forecasting of total remuneration costs is dependent upon the accuracy of profit forecasts. Shareholders will therefore face an increased risk because any cash flow uncertainty reduces the present value of future returns.

(iv)
There are two main aspects of Treasury operations that may create potential risks for NOP's shareholders. The first aspect is the Treasurer's attitude to gearing. It is stated that capital gearing in NOP is low compared to that of its competitors, but this cautious approach may result in a failure to exploit potentially profitable investment opportunities. Finance theory suggests that the cost of debt is below the cost of equity, and so by maintaining a low gearing ratio, NOP is possibly carrying an unnecessarily high weighted average cost of capital, which will reduce the potential profits available to equity.

The second area of Treasury operations that may affect shareholder risks is the company's attitude to hedging. The Treasurer wants all currency exposures exceeding £100,000 to be fully hedged, but in relation to the company's overall revenue, this is a relatively small sum. There is a risk that excessive costs are being incurred in engaging in a substantial number of small external hedging contracts. By centralising hedging management and the use of matching and pooling of risks, the hedging cost could be considerably reduced. Furthermore, the decentralisation of responsibility for currency hedging creates a control risk.

(v)
The company clearly places a high priority on its social and environmental policies, but although such policies may raise NOP's reputation, they can also create some increased risks for shareholders. As already indicated, the agreement to comply with an ethical code requires the introduction of schemes to monitor and manage that compliance. Such systems may be costly and increase shareholder risk. Similarly, the production of a social and environmental report is costly, particularly if full audit procedures are followed.

In declaring a target of zero waste to landfill by 2008, NOP is potentially creating a problem for itself. Although the idea may sound very good and potentially raise the image of NOP, this is an ambitious target, and failure to meet it would damage its reputation and add to shareholder risk. The company needs to think about the potential value versus the additional risks that are added by such a commitment, and be aware that its promise may mean that shareholder risks are increased.

(b)

Report to Board of Directors

Author: Management Accountant

Subject: Risks arising from the recent fall in share price and proposals for possible responses to stimulate price recovery

Risk ownership
Risk ownership at Board level is a mechanism that is used to control a company's key risks. With the introduction of formal risk management systems, most organisations now maintain a key risk register. This register contains a list of the main risks which by their nature and scope are considered to be major threats to the business. One example of a key risk might be IT systems failure in a web based retailer. Such a failure would mean it could not trade and the costs in terms of lost revenues could be huge, even if the systems failure is short lived.

In order for each key risk to be effectively managed, a control system needs to be put in place that identifies lines of responsibility for the monitoring and evaluation of the risk, and the implementation of corrective procedures if the risk is crystallised. Adopting the principle of risk ownership at Board of Director level means that each key risk is owned by an executive director, who takes full responsibility for its management, and reports regularly to the Board on the effectiveness of the control systems. The owner of the risk provides assurance to the Board that the risk monitoring, evaluation and management is running according to plan.

Risk ownership by an executive director does not mean that the day to day management of that risk is in his/her hands. It simply means that this individual is ultimately answerable for ensuring that effective management systems have been put in place. The executive director will therefore tend to devolve responsibility down the management chain, but play an active role in monitoring that the controls are working effectively across the organisation.

The principle of risk ownership at Board of Director level is a vital form of control because it reinforces the idea the risk management needs to be supported from the top of an organisation, but that the control system must be able to track the risk management process from the top through to the bottom. Any de-coupling of controls between Board level and operational levels increases the possibility that a risk may be crystallised. In practice, therefore, it is very important to ensure that risk ownership at Board level exists in practice as well as in name. Where the latter is true, then risk management will not be very effective.

Risks created by the fall in share price
The recent fall in share price poses risks not just for current equity investors but also for the NOP Group. The biggest potential risk comes from the fact that if the market capitalisation falls too low, it may fall below the market value of the net business assets. If this occurs, then NOP will become vulnerable to a take-over bid, because the poor share price will grant an acquirer the scope to buy assets at a discount. The data in the question is insufficient to facilitate a comparison of the market value of equity to the market value of the net assets, but the price is below the level of 2006 and a price falling more rapidly than that of the competition is not a good sign.

A falling share price also creates opportunities for speculators who do not wish to mount a take-over bid, but want to make gains on a general upswing in share prices. Such speculative activity creates share price volatility, and therefore increases the beta value for the Group. A higher beta implies a higher cost of capital, which adds to the risks of the Group.

A company's broader image in the market place can also be affected by its share price, because it can imply that it is facing problems. This can create a destructive cycle in which the share price falls, leading to a weaker corporate image but that weaker image in turn causes a further fall in the share price. The cycle needs to be halted before excessive damage is done.

Finance Director's proposal
The Finance Director holds the view that the falling share price can be corrected via a cost cutting exercise which will result in higher margins and an improvement in shareholder returns. A reduction in production and transportation costs of 5% would cut the cost of goods sold by 3.75%, and the proposed savings in employee costs would boost profit margins by a substantive 6% of sales value. The overall impact on net profit could therefore be substantial and in theory, even if the Price:Earnings ratio was unchanged, the share price would move upwards again. The Finance Director's proposals would only serve to halt the share price fall, however, if its main cause is investor concerns over NOP's relatively poor profitability. If the causes of the share price fall are more complex, or related to specific issues such as a loss of confidence in the CEO or rumours of fraud or false accounting, then even extensive cost cutting will not resolve the situation.

At the same time, the cost-cutting proposals could increase risks for NOP, because the cuts are targeted at core areas of the business where such savings could have a detrimental impact upon product quality. Given that NOP targets the middle to higher price end of the fashion market, and its brands are an important element of its marketing strategy, reduced production costs could lower quality and threaten brand integrity. The area where this risk is perhaps greatest is that of production, where costs may be lowered by using poorer quality materials or less skilled staff. Lower transportation costs might require NOP to be more flexible in its delivery scheduling, either for inward or outward deliveries, or possibly both. Such flexibility could potentially result in production delays or stock-outs which would increase costs and damage the Group's reputation.

Employee costs in Europe are a specific target for cost cutting by the Finance Director because they are 50% above the industry average. There is a risk for NOP in assuming that it should achieve costs which match the industry average, because it is marketing above average cost products. Staff training levels may need to be higher, as well as salaries, in order to achieve sales in the target market, and comparing salaries to the average is too simplistic an approach. In other words, cheaper but less qualified staff may lead to reduced sales, so that the overall impact of the cost-cutting exercise on net profit is negative rather than positive. This is not to say that no employee cost savings are possible, but the additional risks of this policy must be recognised.

At a Group level, there is a risk that its reputation amongst both consumers and shareholders may be tarnished by the news of large scale cost-cutting exercises. If there are large scale redundancies, this can have political repercussions which may not help the Group's desire to adopt a socially responsible image. Similarly, if it shifts production to cheap "sweatshops" it risks the threat of accusations of unethical practices which would again be contrary to its desired image. I would therefore suggest that there are substantial risks associated with following the proposals of the Finance Director.

Marketing Director's proposal

The Marketing Director's proposal is focused on the use of advertising to increase global sales of one specific product range with no accompanying sales loss on other ranges. The chosen range carries a gross margin that is above the average for the group, and so additional sales could work to boost the overall rate of return for NOP. If, for example, glamour range sales can be increased to £1,248 million (the equivalent of 40% of 2006 sales), then, if the existing 22% margin on glamour products is maintained, this would yield £275 million. In other words, the Group's gross margin is increased by £172 million to £640 million, a rise of 36.75%.

In terms of gross margins, the proposal appears to be excellent, but there are risks that the higher gross margin will be eroded by high advertising costs if top film stars are to be used in the advertising campaign. The risk is that whilst both sales and gross returns improve, the net profit falls because of the additional costs incurred by the new advertising. This risk can be managed relatively easily by detailed project planning, and so it can be reduced but not totally eliminated. The risk cannot be eliminated because it is difficult to produce totally accurate forecasts of the impact of advertising upon sales.

Conclusion

In comparing the two proposals, the business philosophy that underpins each of them is very different. The Finance Director's cost cutting response is a defensive one, whilst the Marketing Director's response is an aggressive one. The most suitable option is that which best fits the risk appetite of the Board of Directors, and whilst cost cutting offers potentially more certainty of returns, it also carries higher risks to reputation and corporate image. It also perhaps implies that the Group is in some difficulty and this is not a good message to send to the capital market. In contrast, the more positive advertising and sales route out of trouble carries lower risks but perhaps less chance of success. The Board must therefore weigh up the relative merits of the two proposals and select the one which best fits its current risk appetite.

Exam Q & As

At the time of publication there are no exam Q & As available for the 2010 syllabus. However, the latest specimen exam papers are available on the CIMA website. Actual exam Q & As will be available free of charge to CIMA students on the CIMA website from summer 2010 onwards.